238

FOR ORGANS, PIANOS & ELECTRONIC KEYBOARDS

Twenty Christmas Songs

E-Z Play TODAY chord notation is designed for playing **standard chord positions** or **single key chords** on all **major brand organs** and **electronic keyboards**.

A Joint Publication of  Music Publishers, New York, New York

and

7777 W. BLUEMOUND RD. P.O. BOX 13819 MILWAUKEE, WI 53213

E-Z Play ® TODAY Music Notation © 1975 by HAL LEONARD PUBLISHING CORPORATION
Copyright © 1989 by THE GOODMAN GROUP and HAL LEONARD PUBLISHING CORPORATION
International Copyright Secured   ALL RIGHTS RESERVED   Printed in the U.S.A.

For all works contained herein:
Unauthorized copying, arranging, adapting, recording or public performance is an infringement of copyright.
Infringers are liable under the law.

E-Z PLAY is a registered trademark of HAL LEONARD PUBLISHING CORPORATION

Twenty Five Top Christmas Songs

Contents

- 4 Blue Christmas
- 6 Carrying The Lord To Jerusalem (Little White Donkey)
- 8 The Christmas Waltz
- 10 C*H*R*I*S*T*M*A*S
- 12 Do You Hear What I Hear
- 18 Frosty The Snow Man
- 15 Have Yourself A Merry Little Christmas
- 20 Here Comes Santa Claus
- 26 A Holly Jolly Christmas
- 28 Home For The Holidays (There's No Place Like)
- 30 I Saw Mommy Kissing Santa Claus
- 32 I'll Be Home For Christmas
- 34 Jingle-Bell Rock
- 36 Last Christmas
- 40 Let It Snow! Let It Snow! Let It Snow!
- 23 The Little Drummer Boy
- 42 Merry, Merry Christmas Baby
- 48 My Favorite Things
- 50 Pretty Paper
- 52 Rudolph The Red-Nosed Reindeer
- 54 Santa Claus Is Coming To Town
- 45 Shake Me I Rattle (Squeeze Me I Cry)
- 56 Silver Bells
- 58 Sleigh Ride
- 60 Suzy Snowflake
- 64 Registration Guide

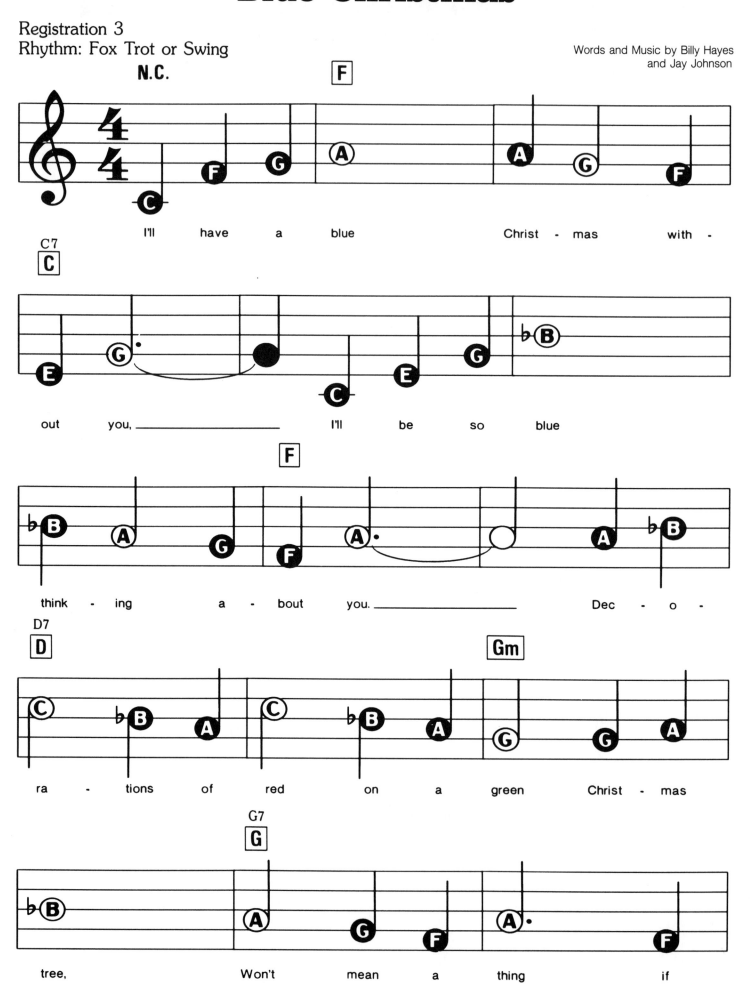

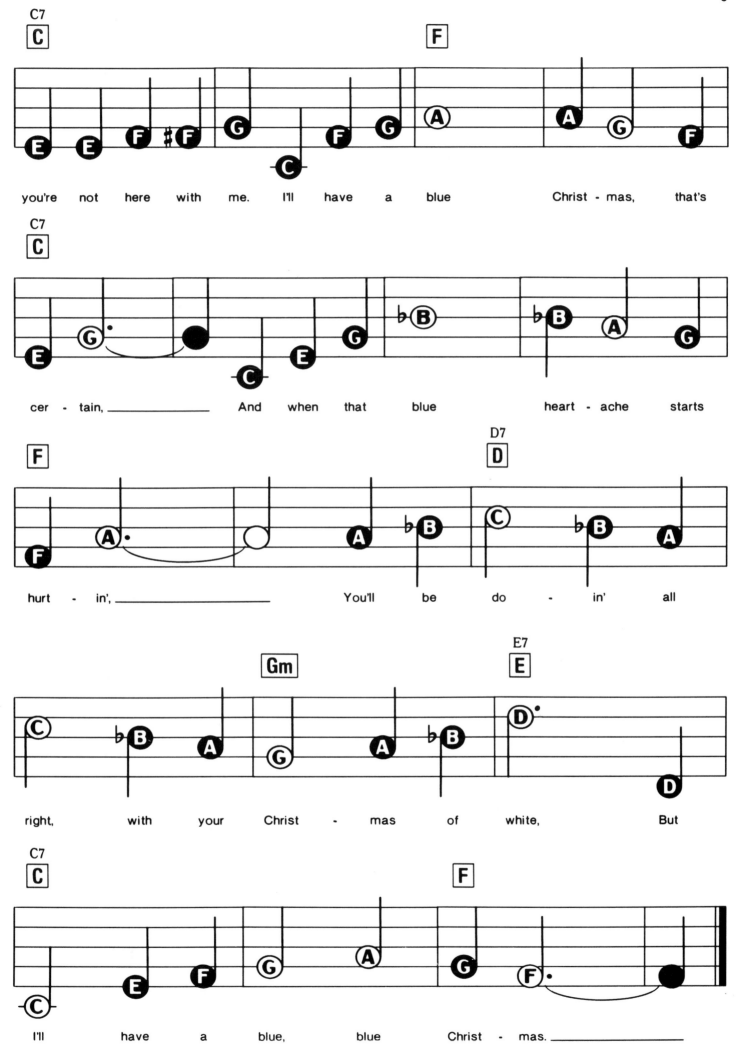

Carrying the Lord To Jerusalem
(Little White Donkey)

Registration 5
Rhythm: March

By Roy C. Bennett

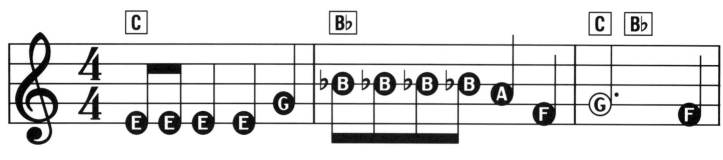

Lit - tle white don - key, Com - ing down the road, clip clop, clip
Shep - herd of man - kind has a mis - sion to ful - fill.
Lit - tle white don - key, when your bless - ed jour - ney's through, clip

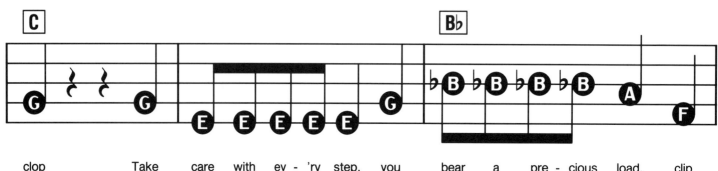

clop Take care with ev - 'ry step, you bear a pre - cious load, clip
         He must show His flock the path to peace and good -
clop. Though you're just a don - key, all men will be bless - ing

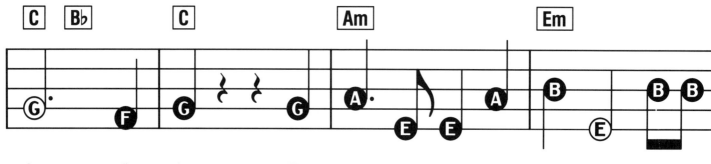

clop, clip clop; The peo - ple shout, "Ho - san - na the Mes -
will.   The peo - ple spread their gar - ments to
you, clip clop. For you're the one He's cho - sen in

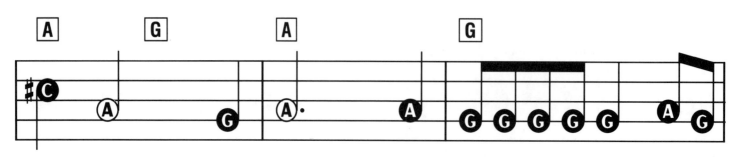

si - ah is come." The rid - er on your back is the
smooth - en your way. You're thirst - y and you're tired, but you
all of Gal - i - lee. Lift up your head and be

Copyright © 1969 by Jewel Music Publishing Co., Inc.
All Rights Reserved

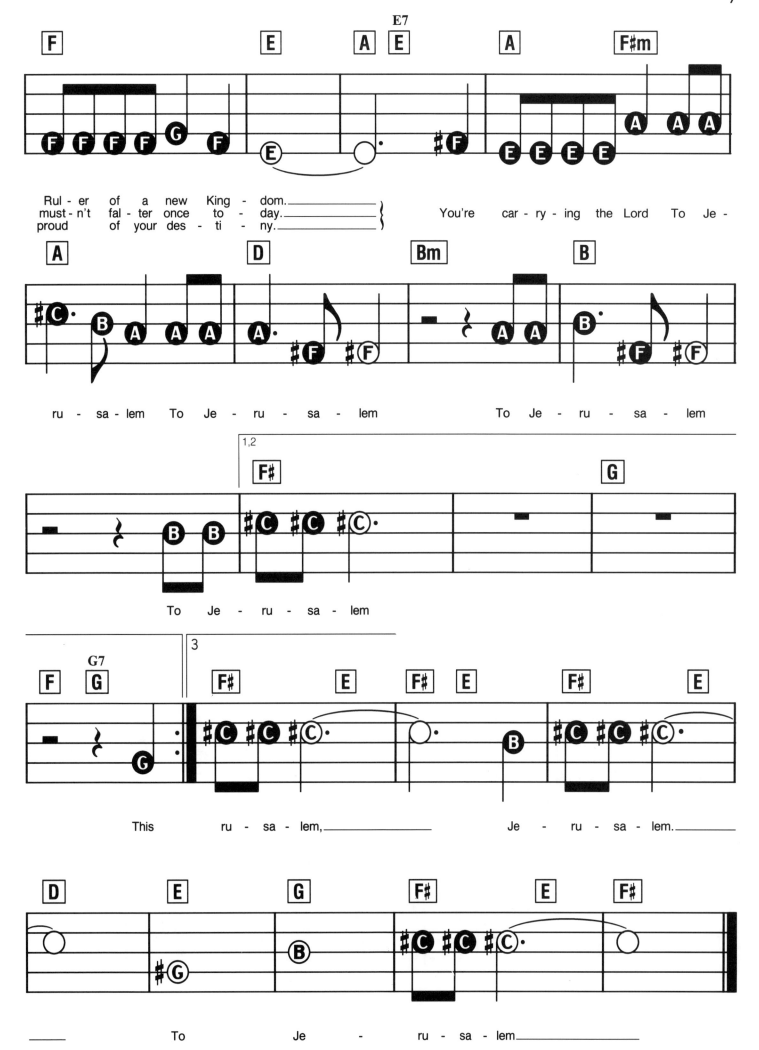

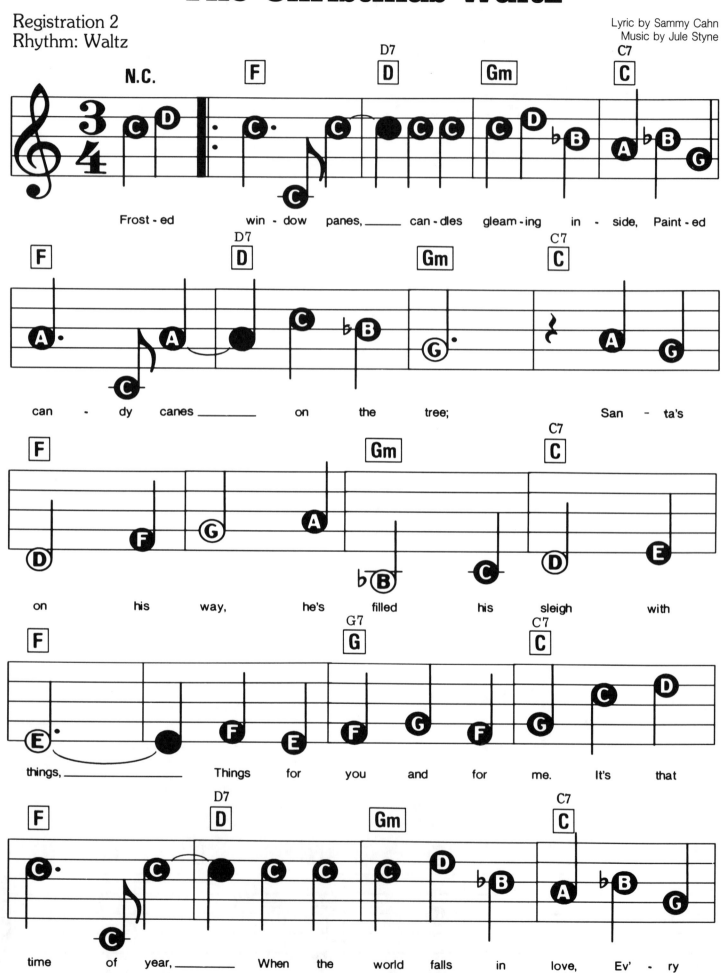

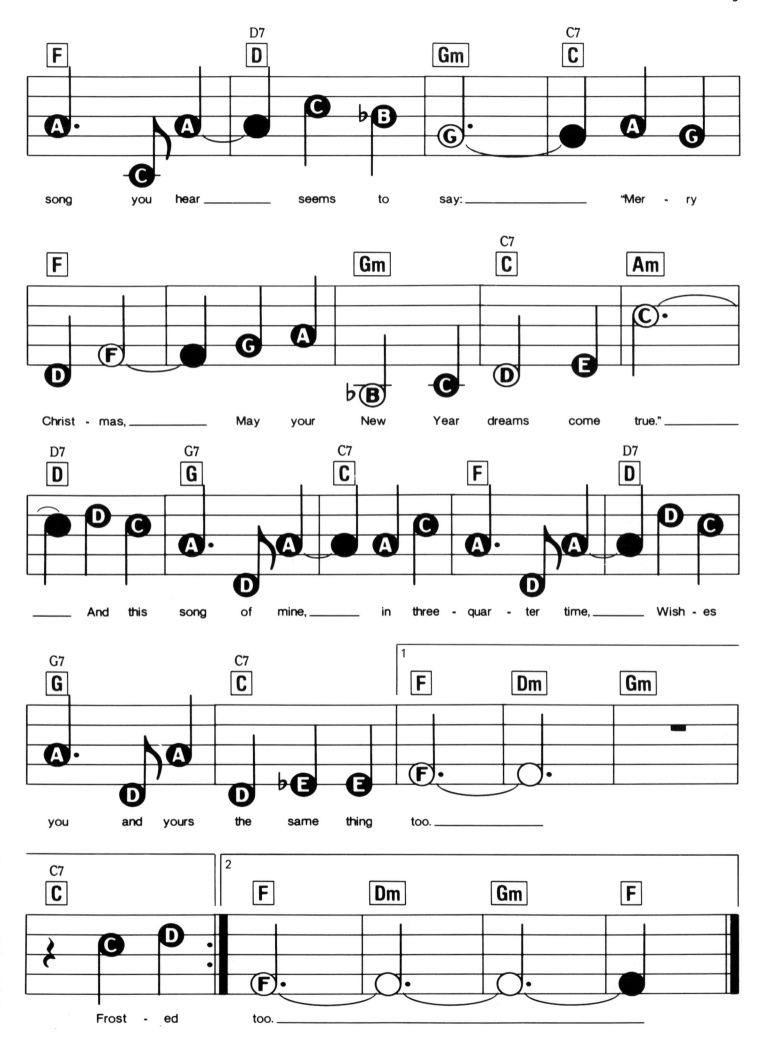

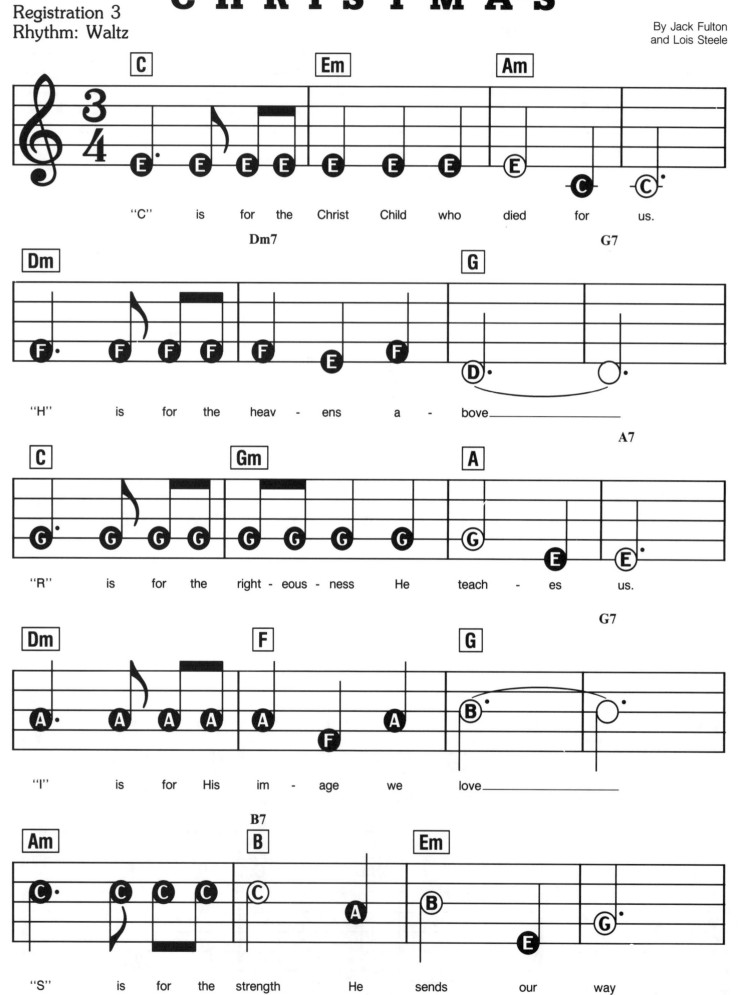

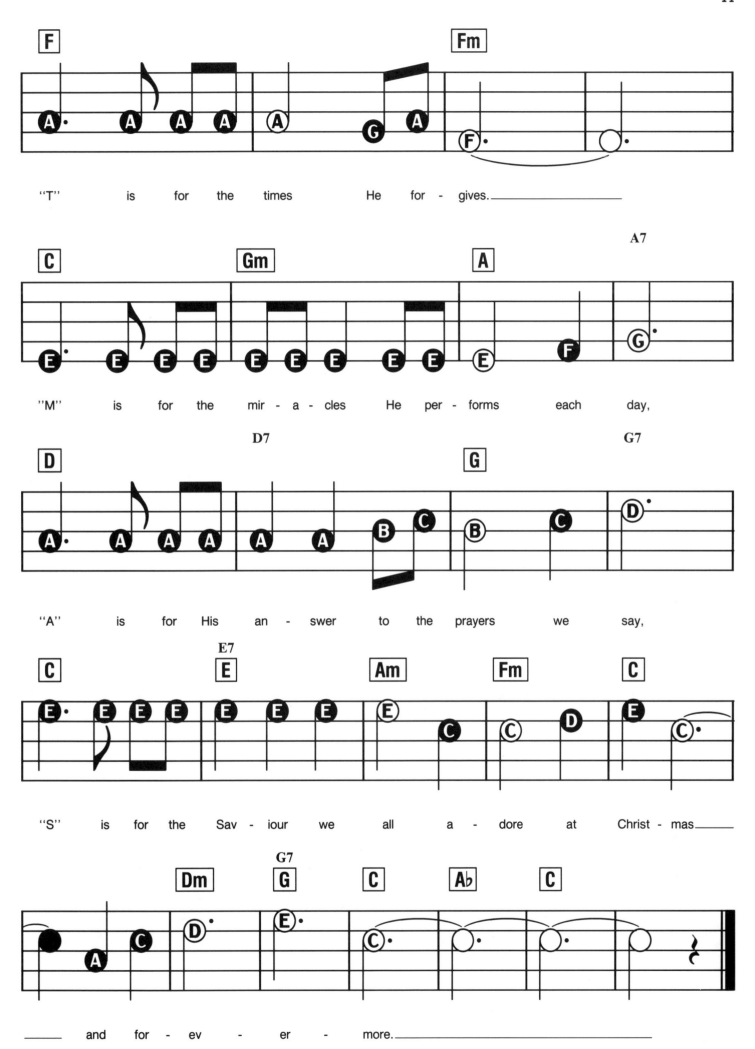

Do You Hear What I Hear

Registration 4

By Noel Regney and Gloria Shayne

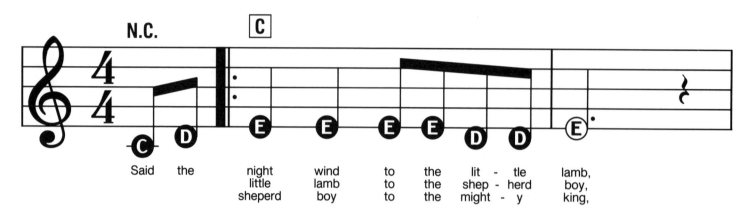

Said the night wind to the lit - tle lamb,
little lamb to the shep - herd boy,
sheperd boy to the might - y king,

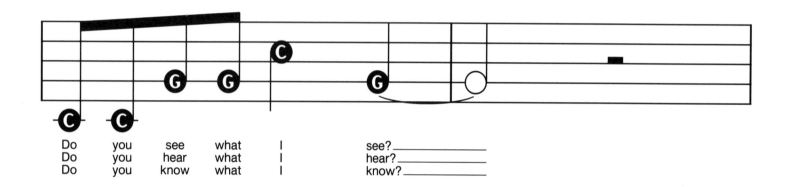

Do you see what I see?_____
Do you hear what I hear?_____
Do you know what I know?_____

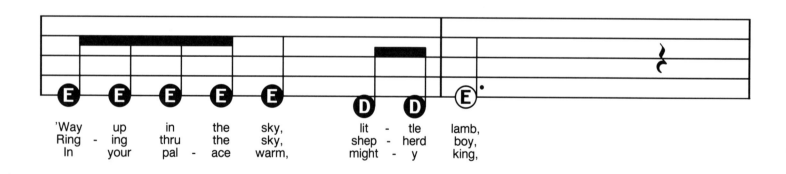

'Way up in the sky, lit - tle lamb,
Ring - ing thru the sky, shep - herd boy,
In your pal - ace warm, might - y king,

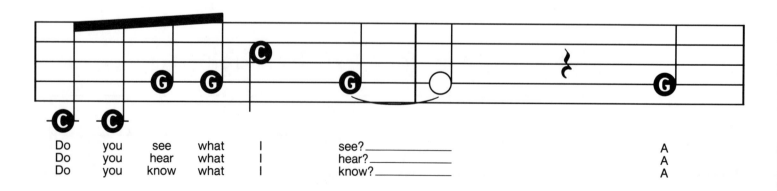

Do you see what I see?_____ A
Do you hear what I hear?_____ A
Do you know what I know?_____ A

Copyright © 1962 by Regent Music Corp.
All Rights Reserved

14

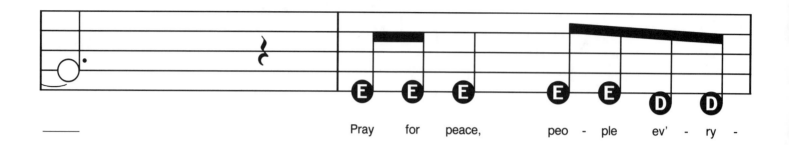

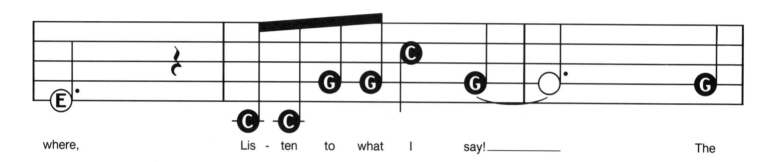

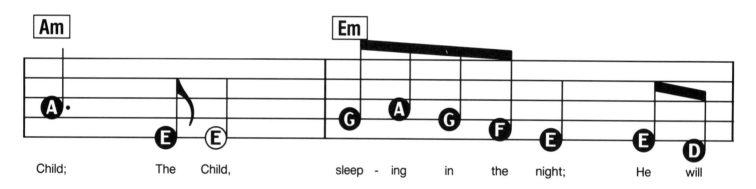

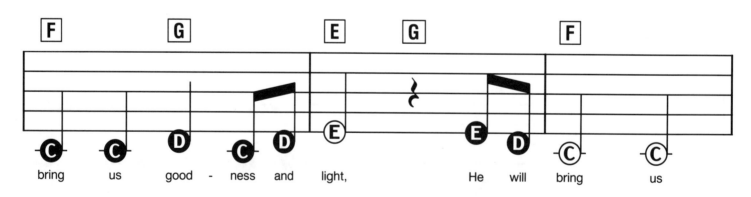

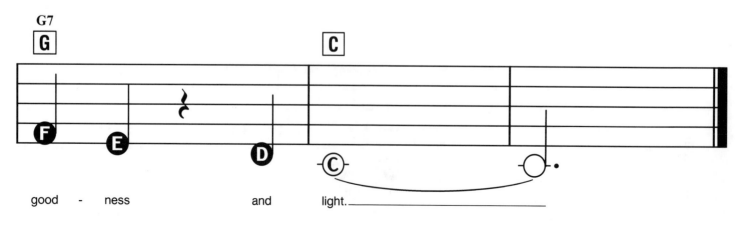

15

Have Yourself A Merry Little Christmas

Registration 7
Rhythm: Swing or Big Band

By Hugh Martin and Ralph Blane

C | Am | Dm G7/G | C Am
C E G C E G F E D C D C E G C

Have your-self a mer-ry lit-tle Christ-mas let your heart be

Dm G7/G | C | Am | Dm G7/G | E7/E A7/A
G E G C E D C B A G F E

light, Next year all our trou-bles will be out of sight.____

D7/D G7/G | C | Am | Dm G7/G
C E G C E G F E D C D

____ Have your-self a mer-ry lit-tle Christ-mas,

C | Am | Dm G7/G | C | Am
C E G C G E G C E

make your Yule-tide gay, Next year all our

Copyright © 1943 (Renewed 1971) Metro-Goldwyn Mayer, Inc.
Copyright © 1944 (Renewed 1972) Leo Feist, Inc.
All Rights for Leo Feist, Inc. assigned to SBK Catalogue Partnership
All Rights Controlled and Administered by SBK Catalogue
International Copyright Secured   Made in U.S.A.   All Rights Reserved

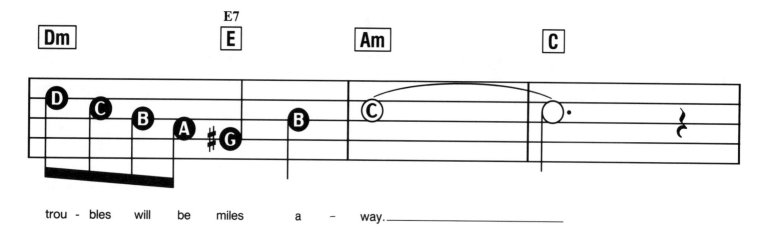
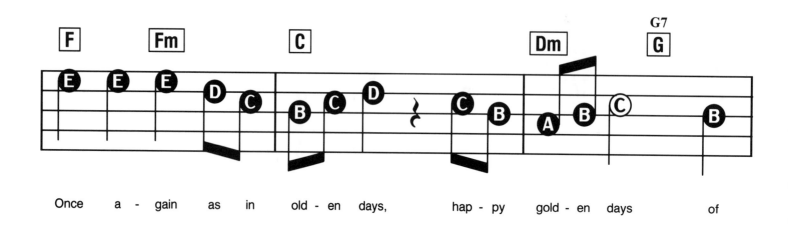
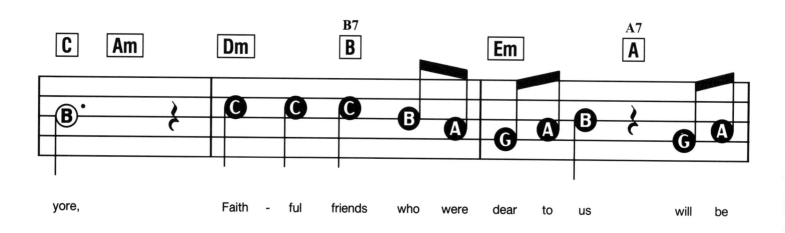
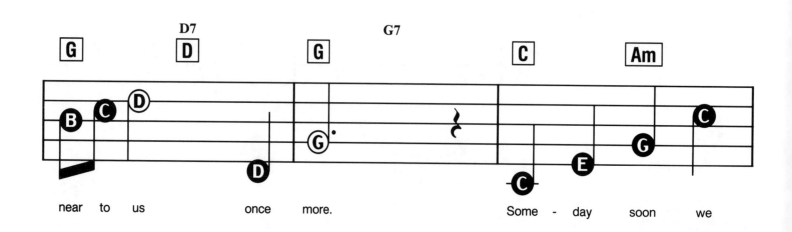

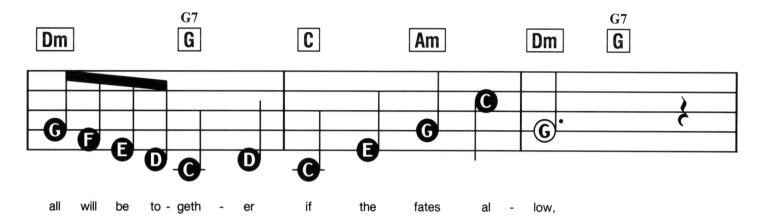
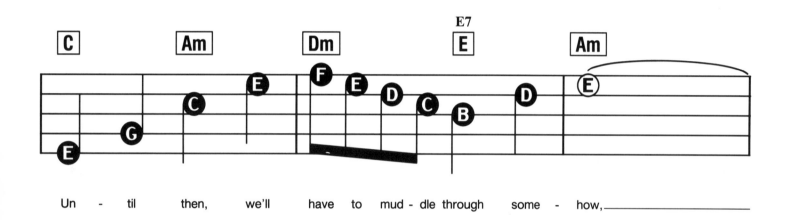
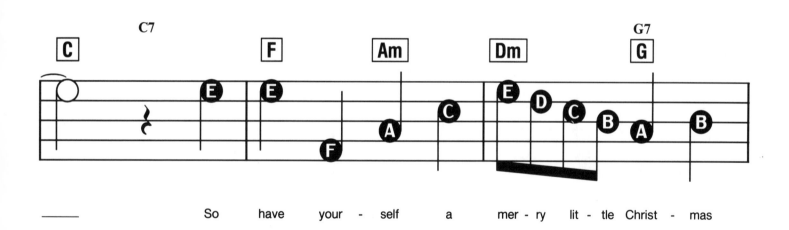
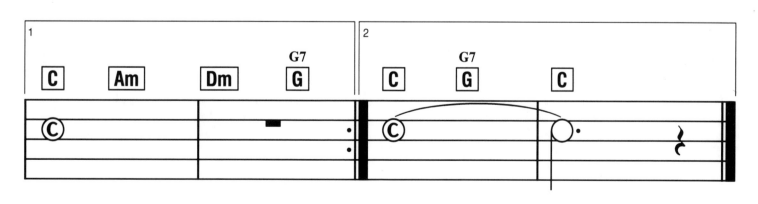

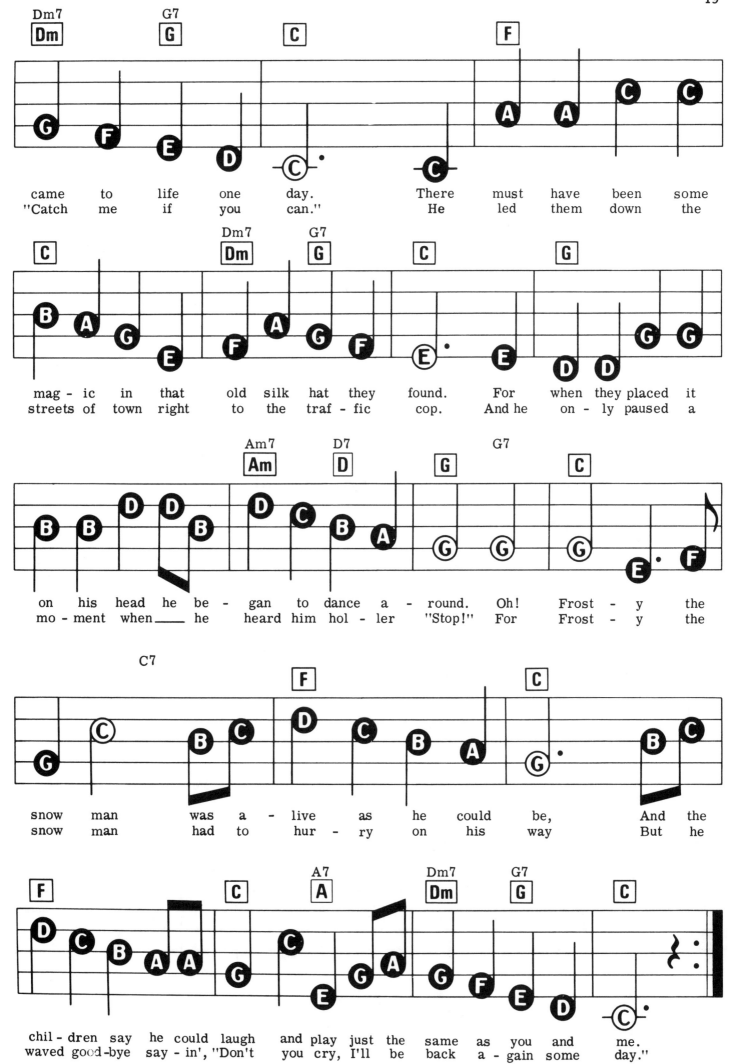

Here Comes Santa Claus

Registration 4
Rhythm: Swing

By Gene Autry and Oakley Haldman

Here comes San - ta Claus! Here comes San - ta Claus! Right down San - ta Claus

Lane!
1. Vix - en and Blitz - en and all his rein - deer are
2. He's got a bag that is all filled with toys for the

pull - ing on the rein. Bells are ring - ing,
boys and girls a - gain. Hear those sleigh - bells

chil - dren sing - ing, all is mer - ry and bright.
jin - gle jan - gle, what a beau - ti - ful sight.

Copyright © 1946 (Renewed) Western Publishing Co.
International Copyright Secured   Made in U.S.A.   All Rights Reserved

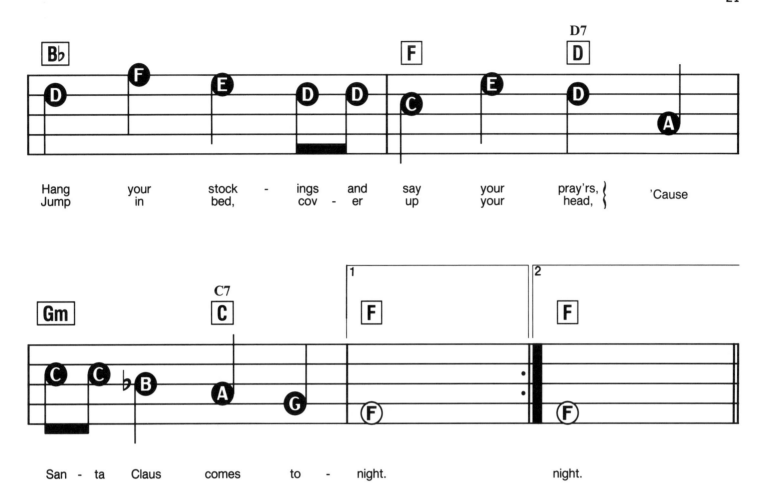
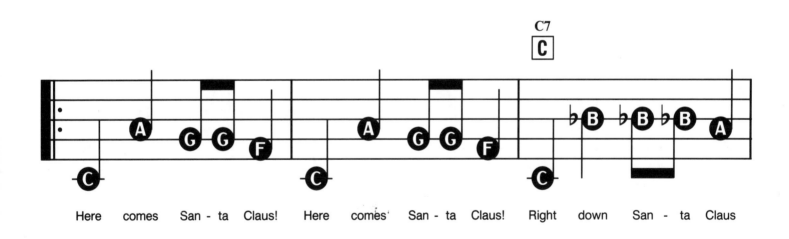
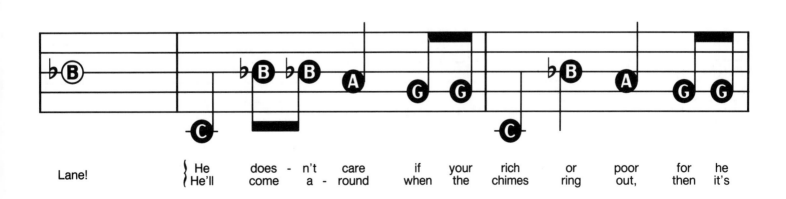

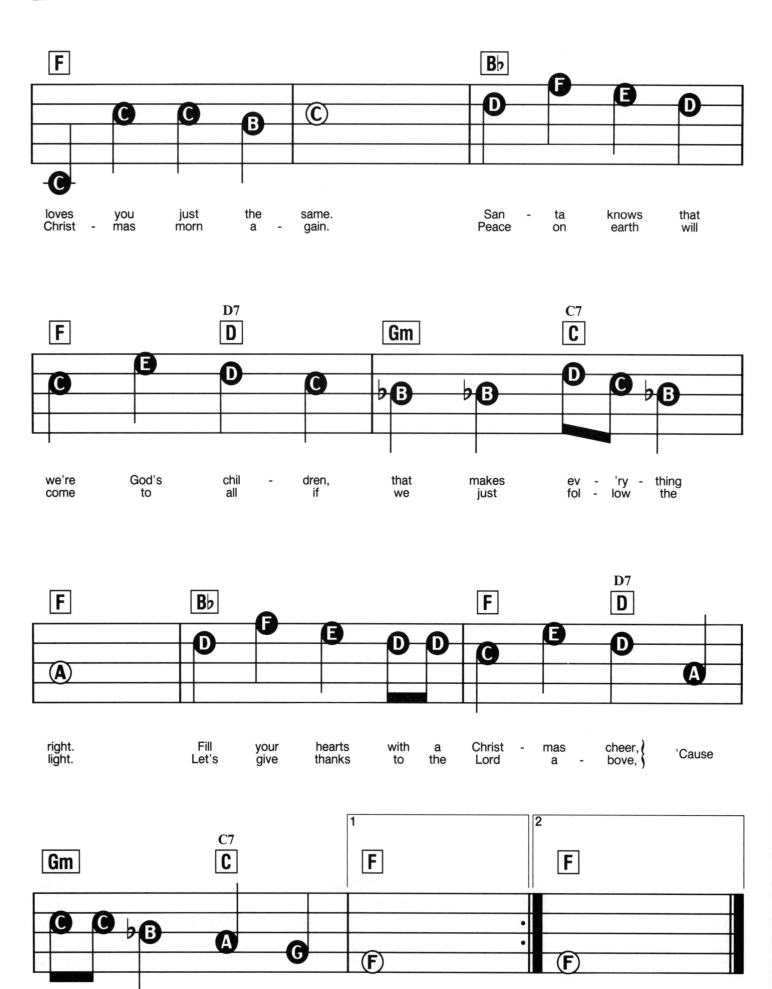

The Little Drummer Boy

Registration 2
Rhythm: March

Words and Music by Katherine Davis,
Henry Onorati and Harry Simeone

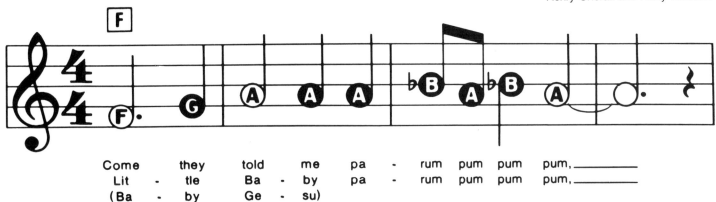

Come they told me pa - rum pum pum pum,_____
Lit - tle Ba - by pa - rum pum pum pum,_____
(Ba - by Ge - su)

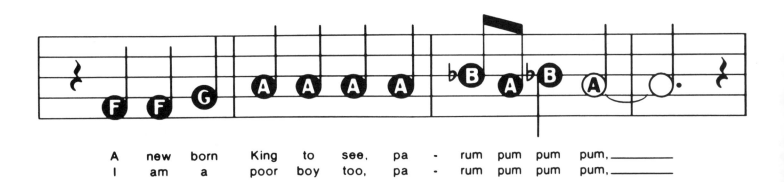

A new born King to see, pa - rum pum pum pum,_____
I am a poor boy too, pa - rum pum pum pum,_____

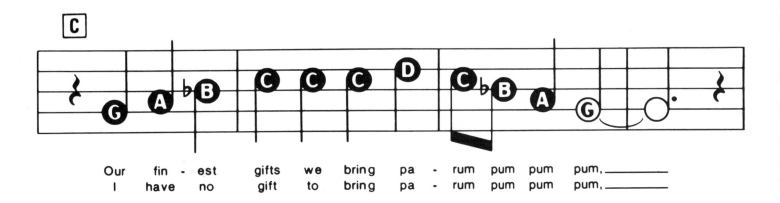

Our fin - est gifts we bring pa - rum pum pum pum,_____
I have no gift to bring pa - rum pum pum pum,_____

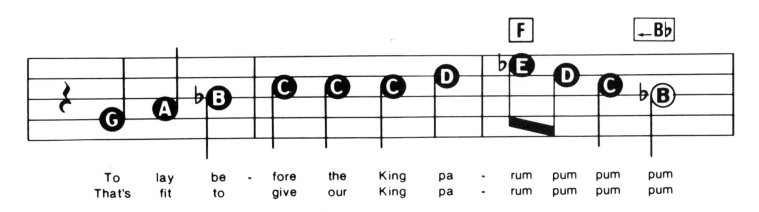

To lay be - fore the King pa - rum pum pum pum
That's fit to give our King pa - rum pum pum pum

Copyright © 1958 by Mills Music, Inc. and International Korwin Corp.
Copyright Renewed.
Used with permission.   All Rights Reserved.

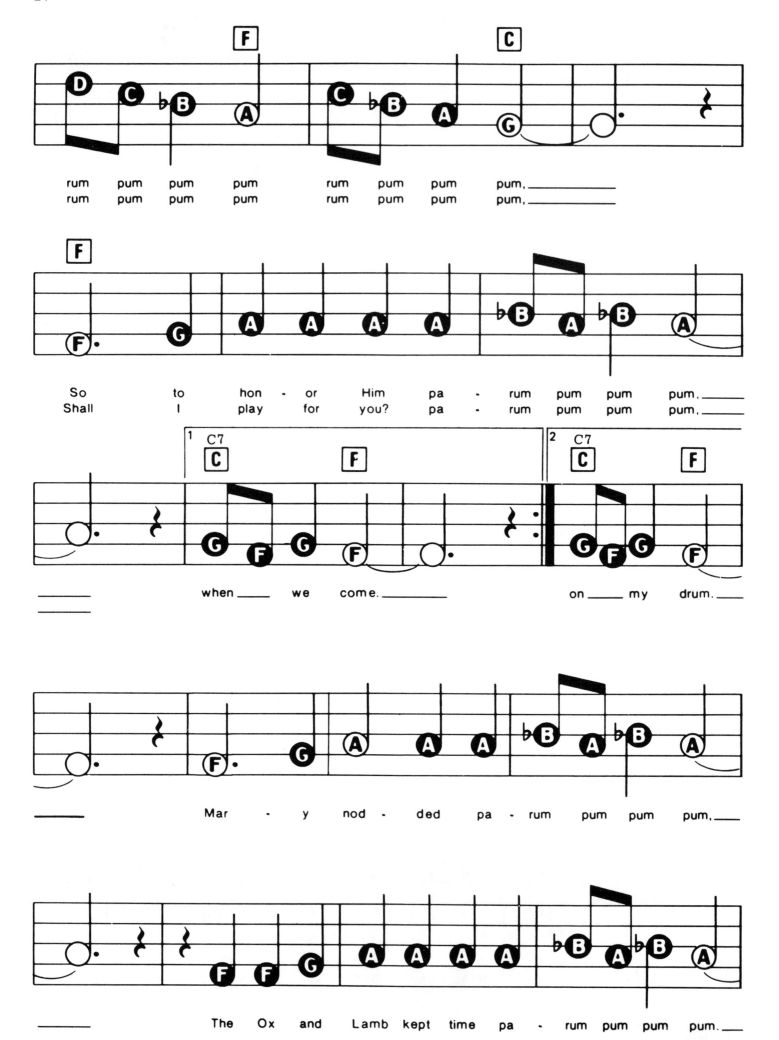

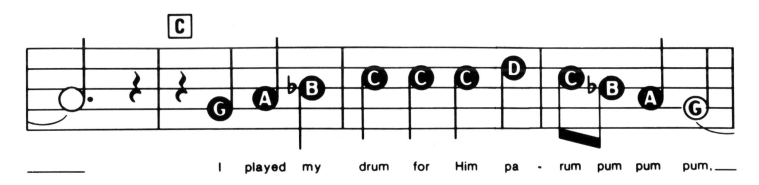
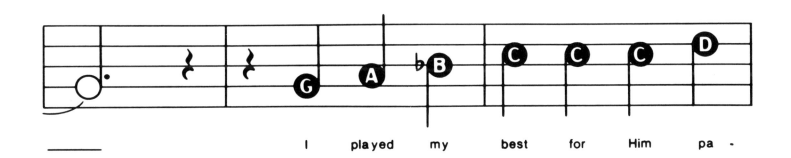
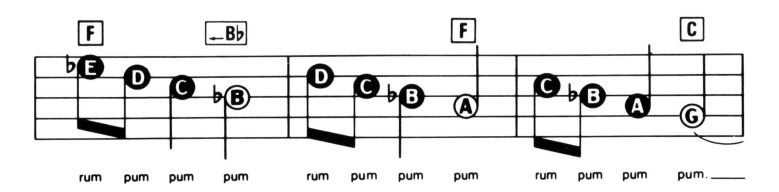
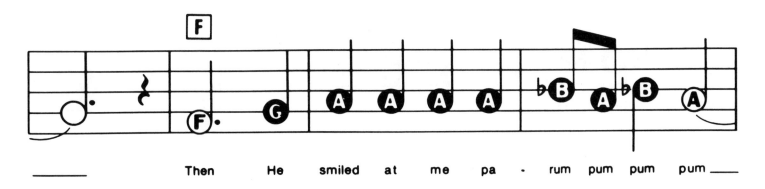
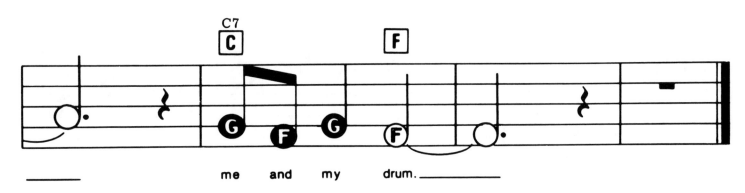

A Holly Jolly Christmas

Registration 9
Rhythm: Swing

Words and Music by
Johnny Marks

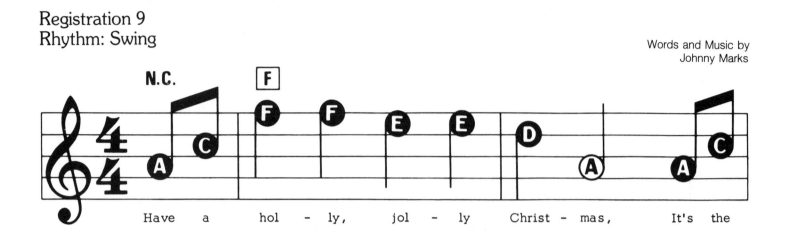

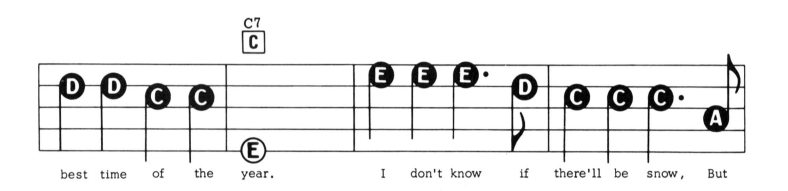

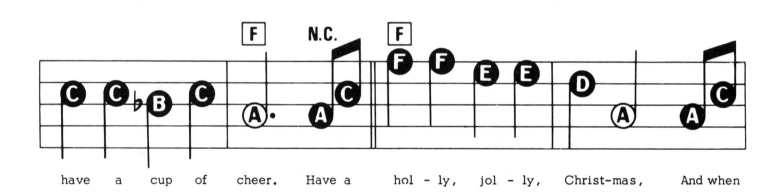

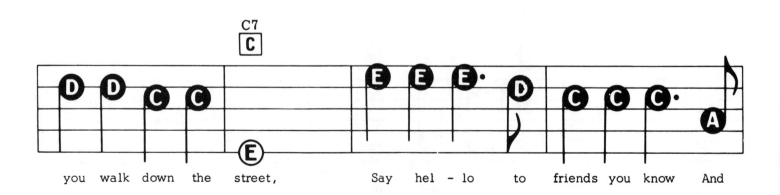

Copyright © 1962 & 1964 by St. Nicholas Music, Inc., 1619 Broadway, New York, New York 10019
All Rights Reserved

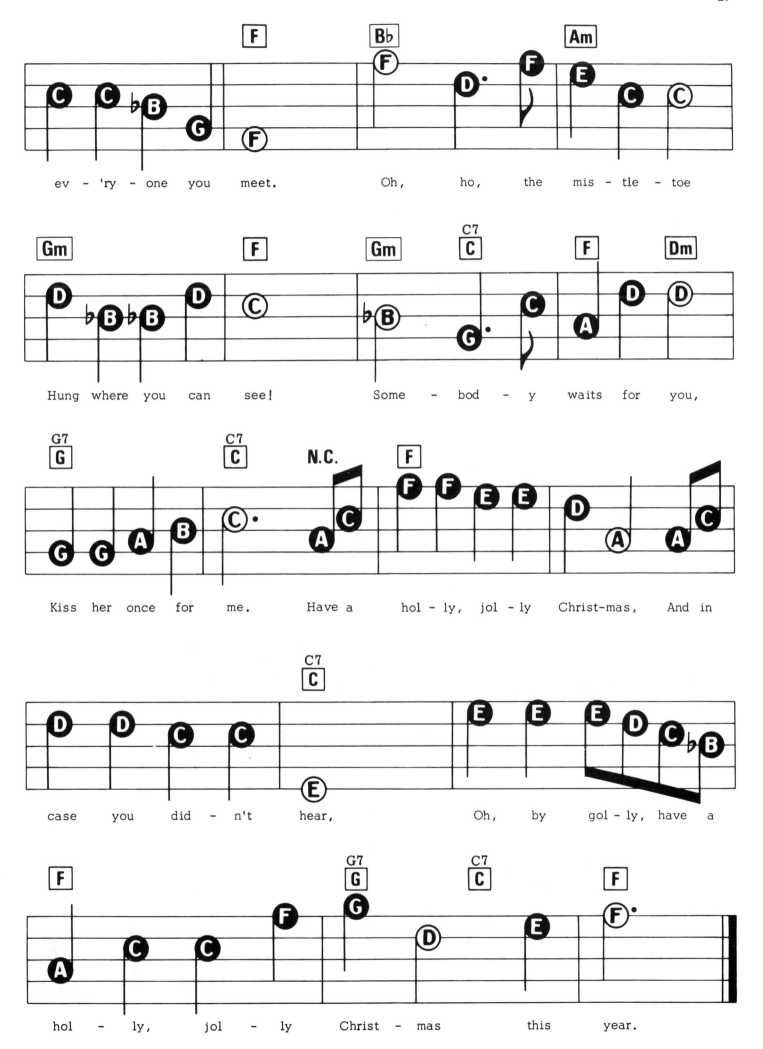

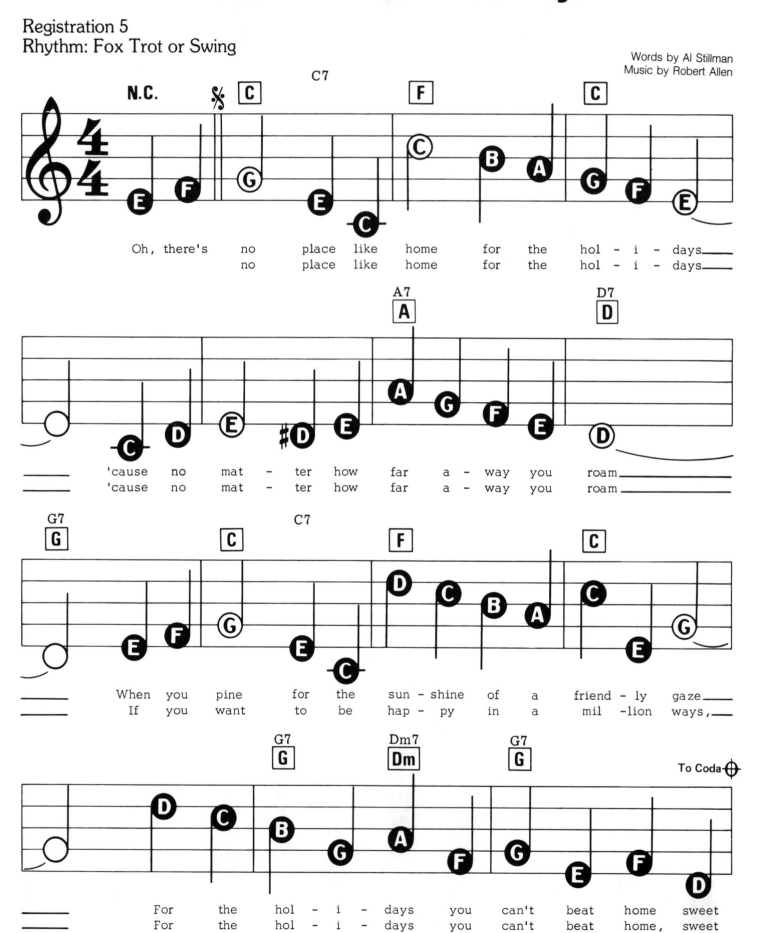

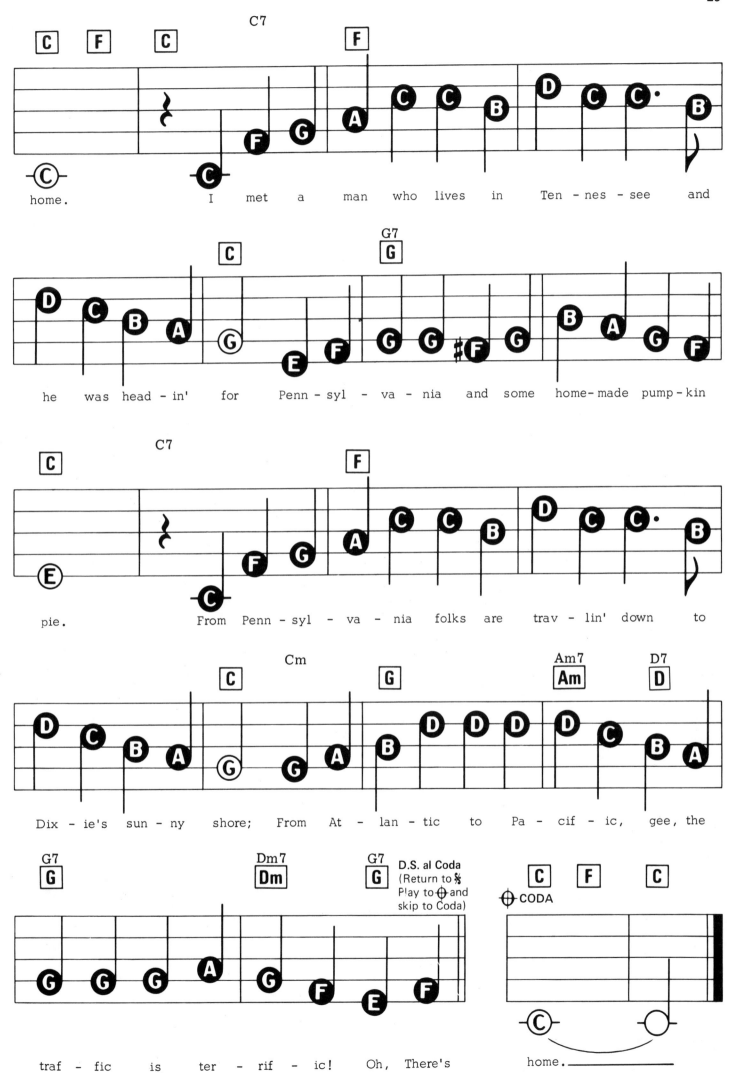

I Saw Mommy Kissing Santa Claus

Registration 5
Rhythm: Fox Trot or Swing

Words and Music by
Tommie Connor

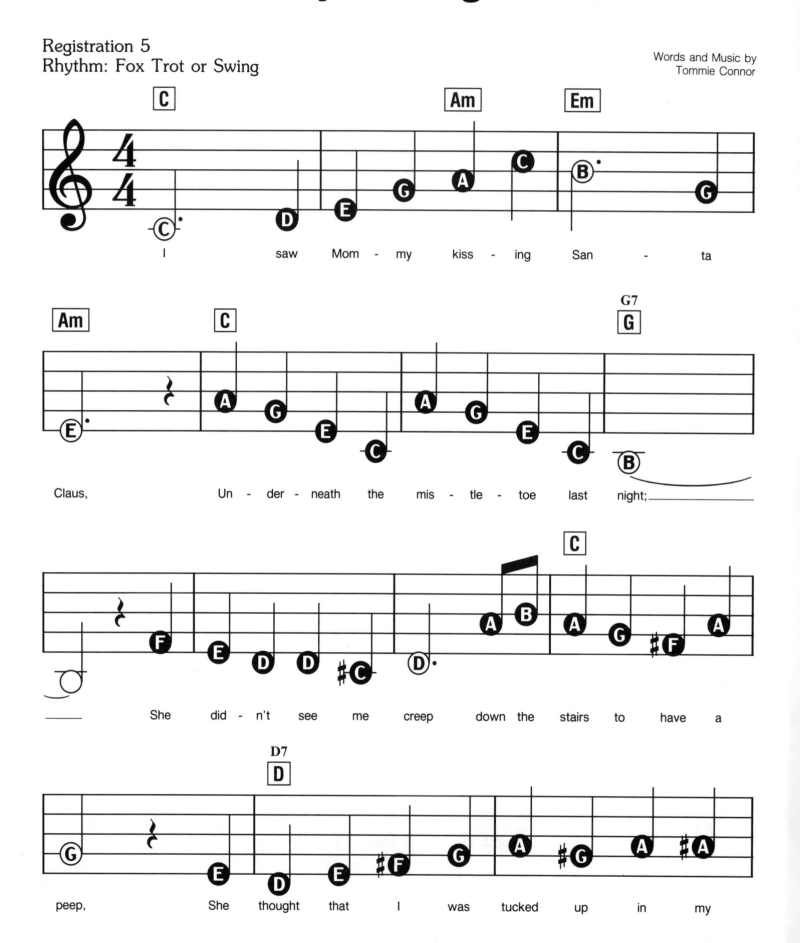

Copyright © 1952 (Renewed) Jewel Music Publishing Co., Inc.
All Rights Reserved

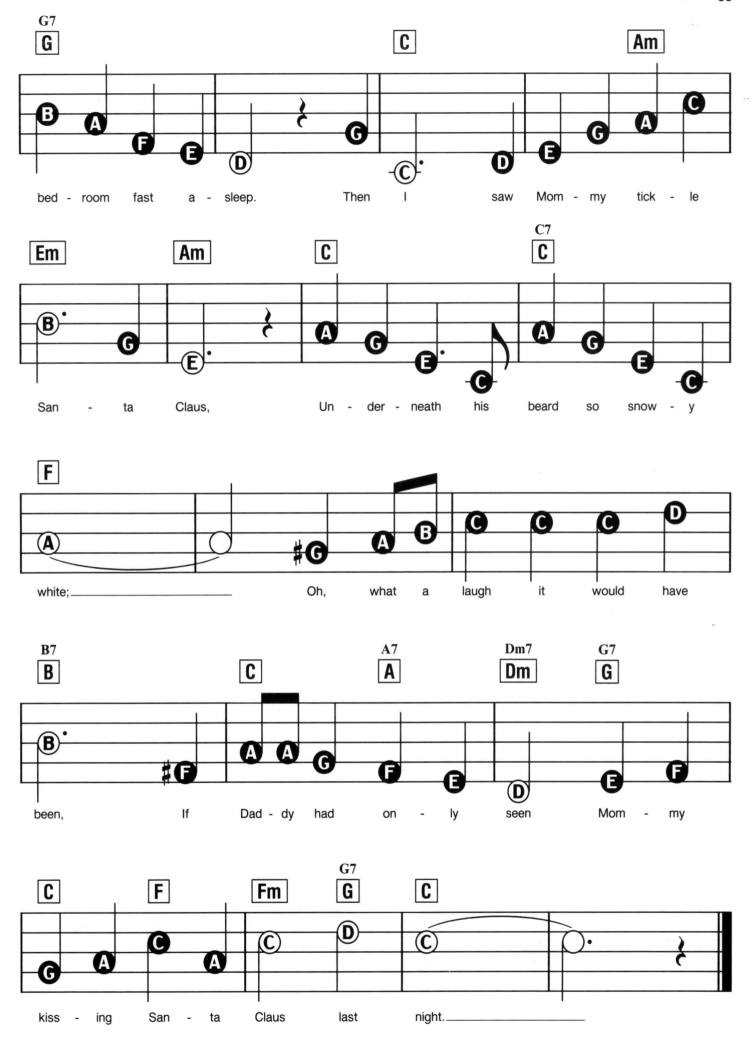

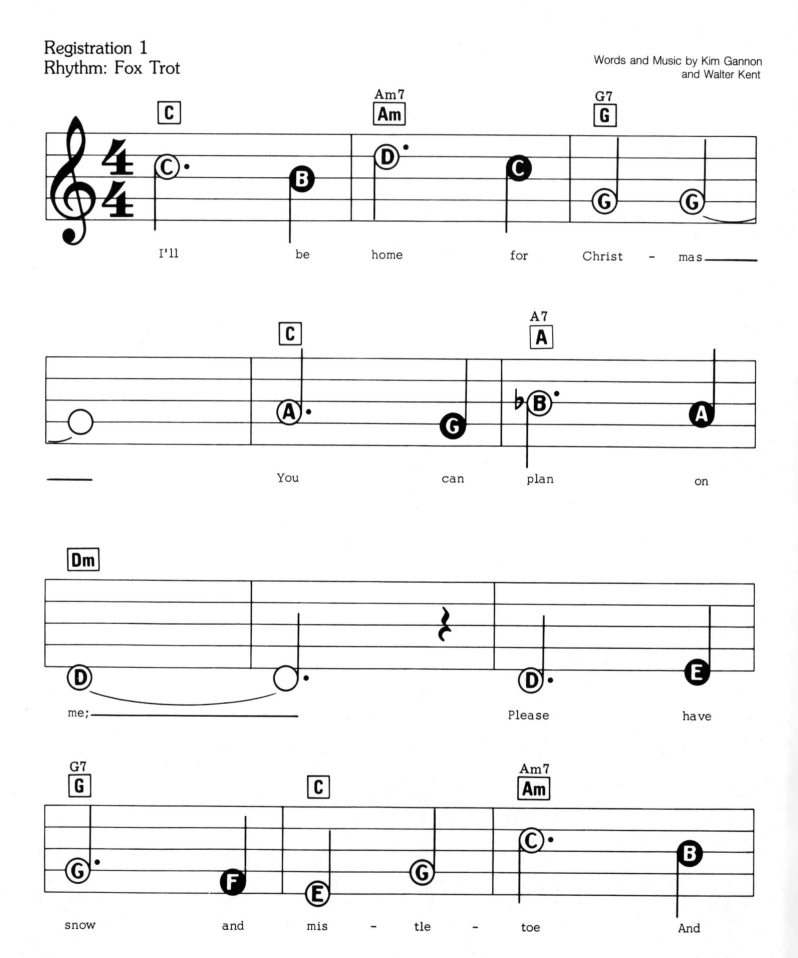

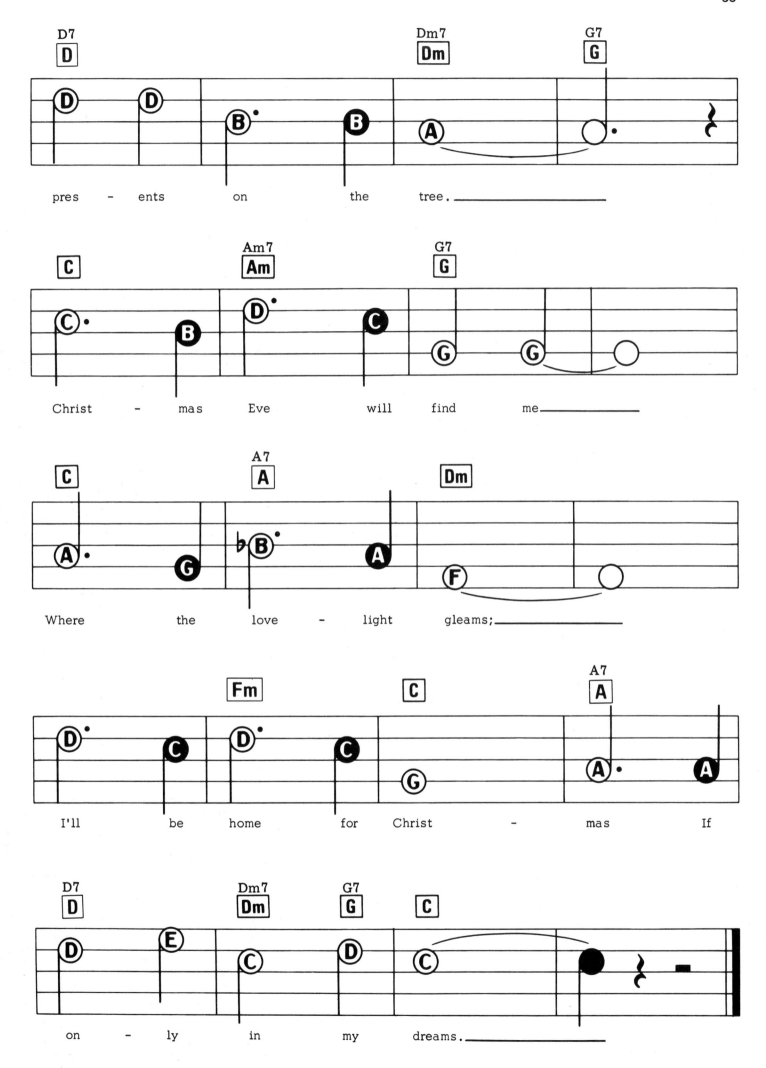

Jingle-Bell Rock

Registration 5
Rhythm: Rock or Fox Trot

Words and Music by Joe Beal
and Jim Boothe

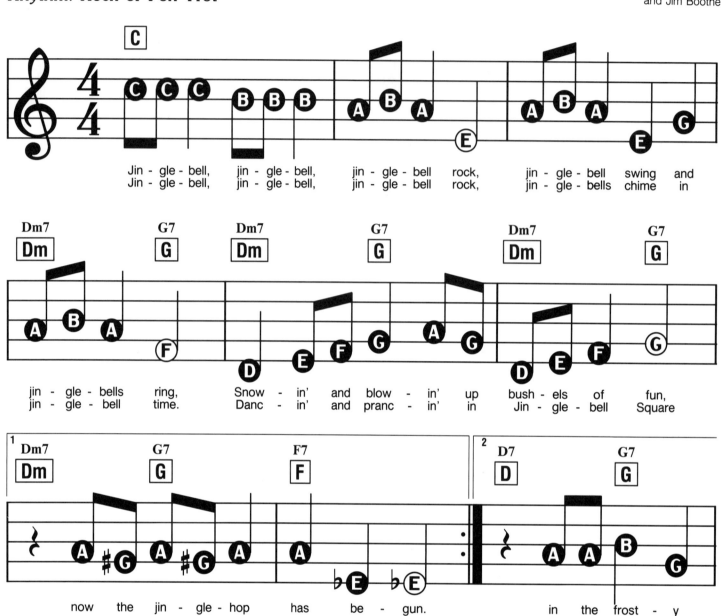

Jin - gle - bell, jin - gle - bell, jin - gle - bell rock, jin - gle - bell swing and
Jin - gle - bell, jin - gle - bell, jin - gle - bell rock, jin - gle - bells chime in

jin - gle - bells ring, Snow - in' and blow - in' up bush - els of fun,
jin - gle - bell time. Danc - in' and pranc - in' in Jin - gle - bell Square

now the jin - gle - hop has be - gun.   in the frost - y

air. What a bright_____ time, it's the right_____ time to

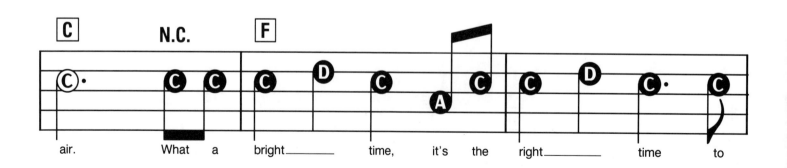

Copyright © 1957 by Cornell Music, Inc.
All Rights controlled by Chappell & Co. (Intersong Music, Publisher)
International Copyright Secured   ALL RIGHTS RESERVED   Printed in the U.S.A.
Unauthorized copying, arranging, adapting, recording or public performance is an infringement of copyright.
Infringers are liable under the law.

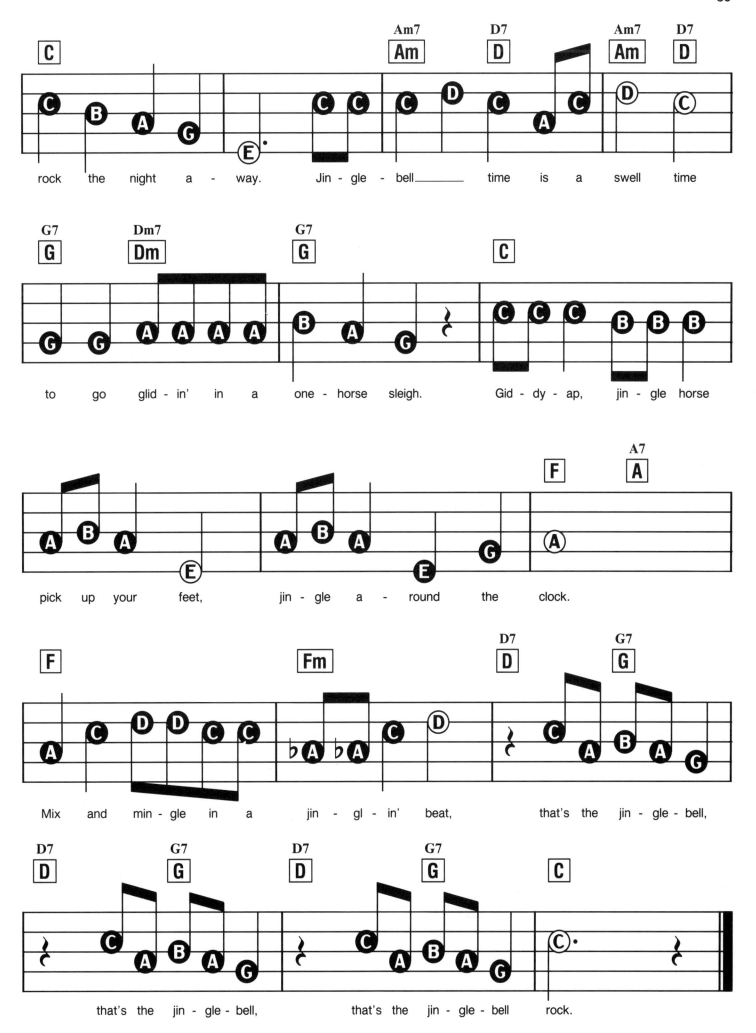

Last Christmas

Registration 1
Rhythm: Disco or 16 Beat

Words and Music by
George Michael

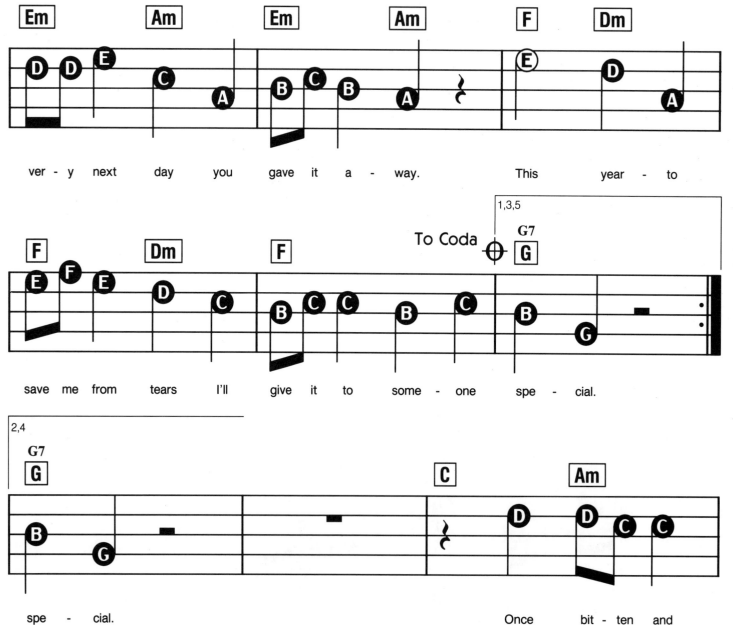

Copyright © 1985 by Morrison-Leahy Music Ltd.
Published in the U.S.A. by Chappell & Co.
International Copyright Secured   ALL RIGHTS RESERVED   Printed in the U.S.A.
Unauthorized copying, arranging, adapting, recording or public performance is an infringement of copyright.
Infringers are liable under the law.

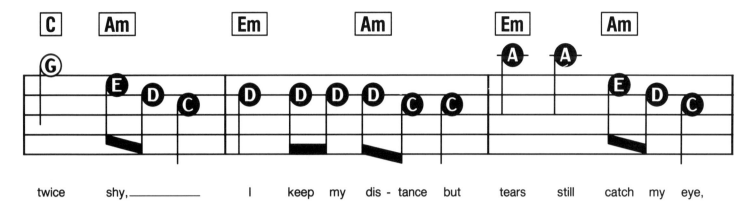
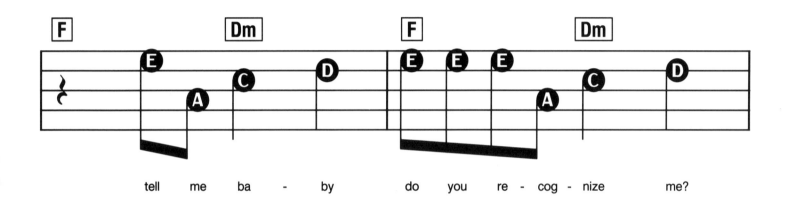
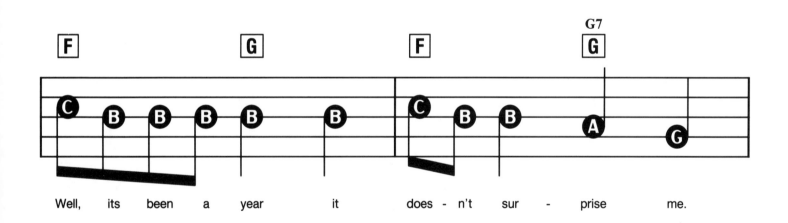
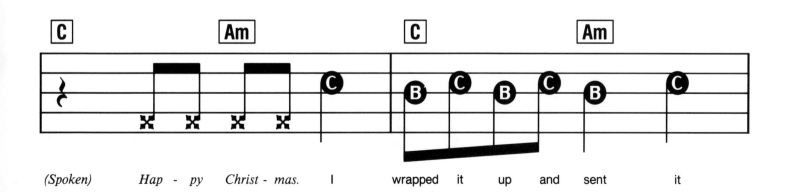

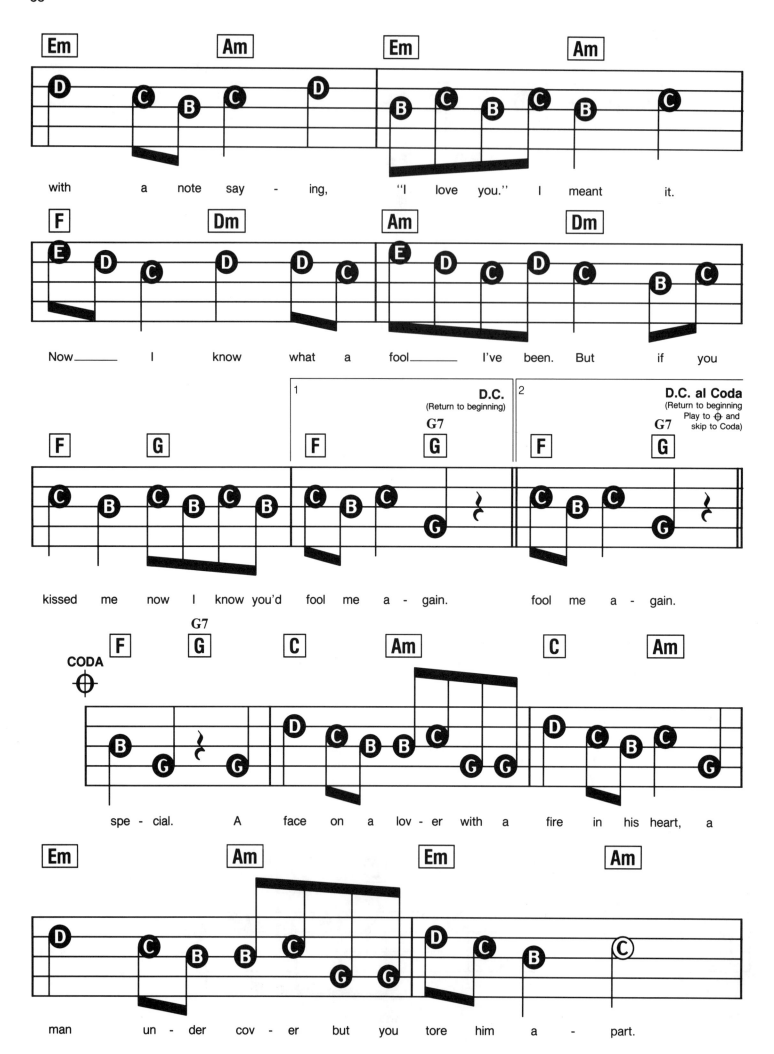

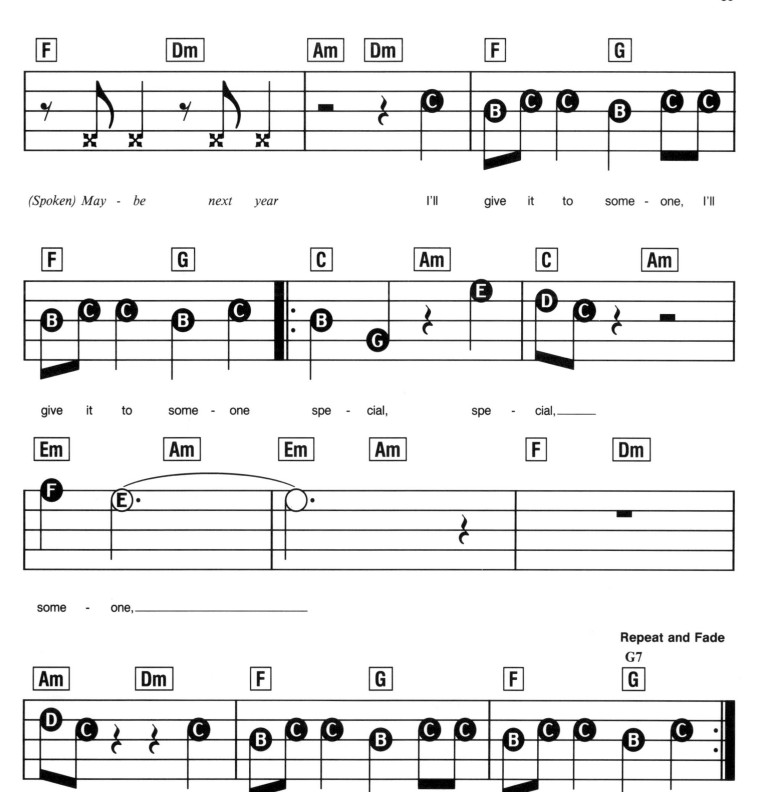

Additional Lyrics

A crowded room, friends with tired eyes.
I'm hiding from you and your soul of ice.
My God, I thought you were someone to rely on.
Me, I guess I was a shoulder to cry on.
A face on a lover with a fire in his heart,
A man under cover but you tore me apart.
Oo, now I've found a new love.
You'll never fool me again.

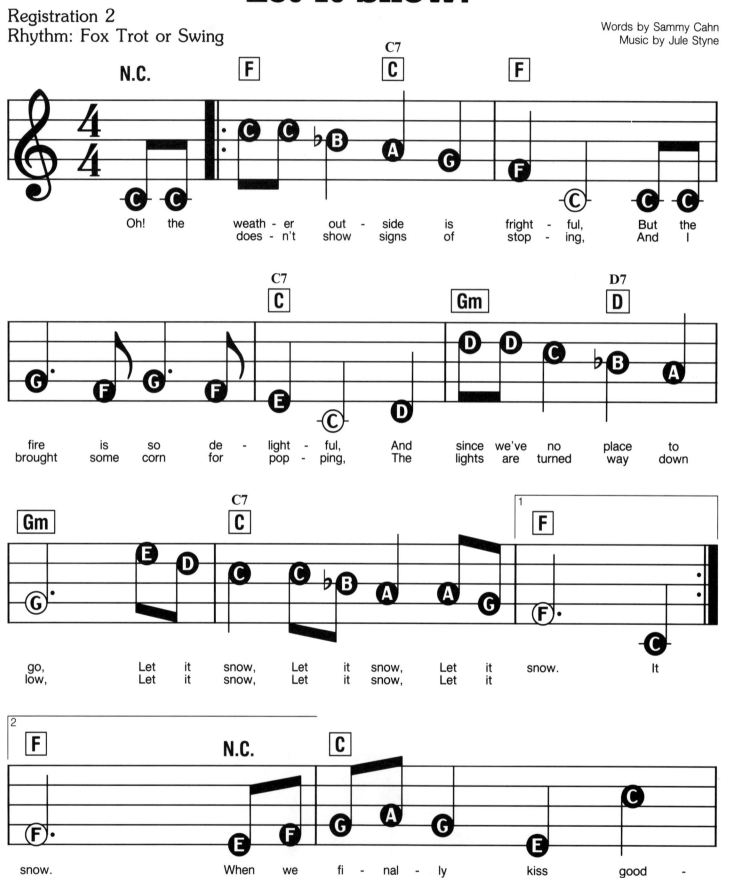

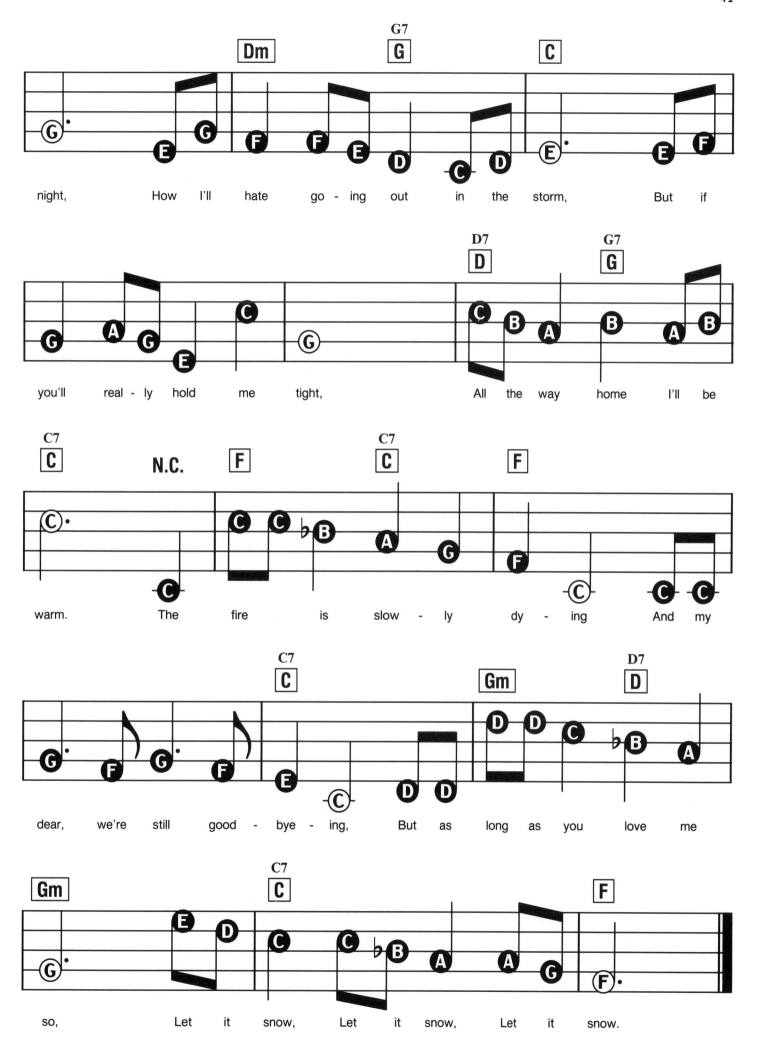

Merry, Merry Christmas Baby

Registration 2
Rhythm: Slow Rock

By Margo Sylvia and Gil Lopez

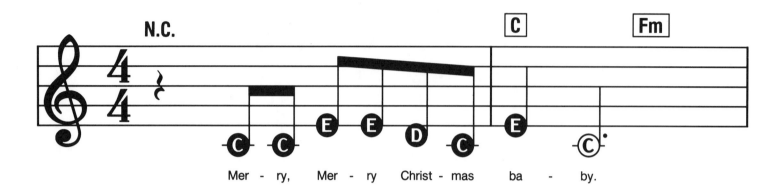

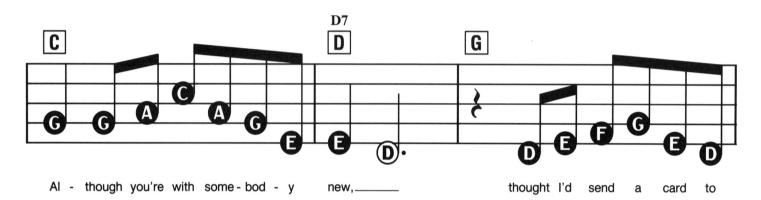

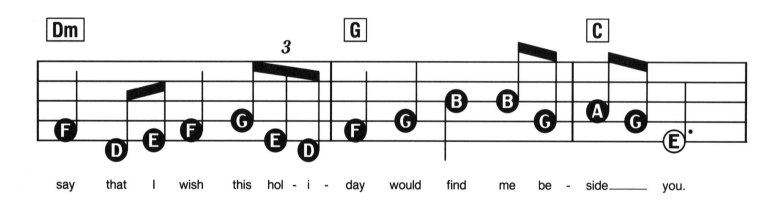

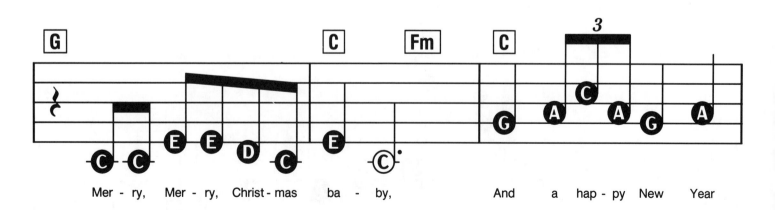

Copyright © 1956, 1957 (Renewed) by Arc Music Corp.
All Rights Reserved

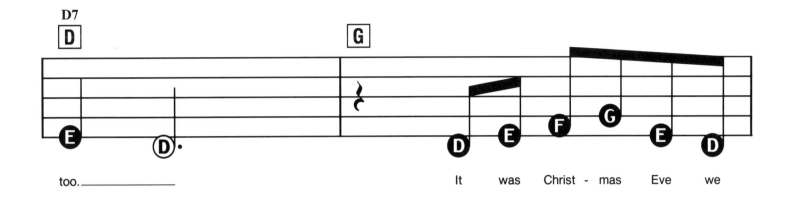
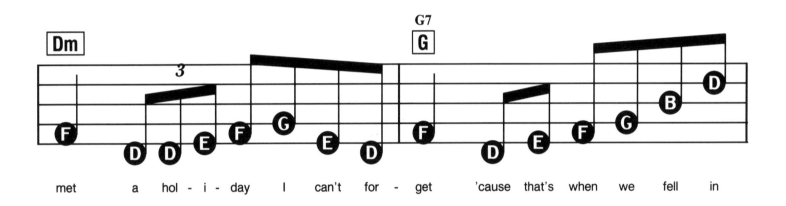
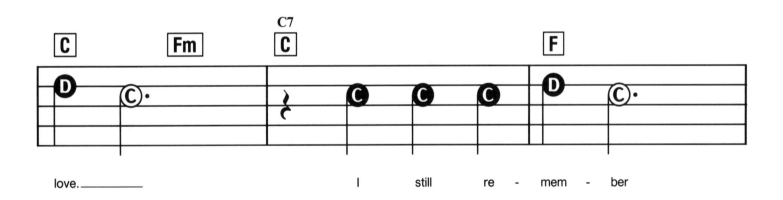
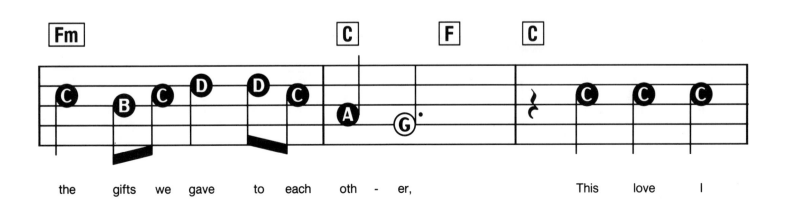

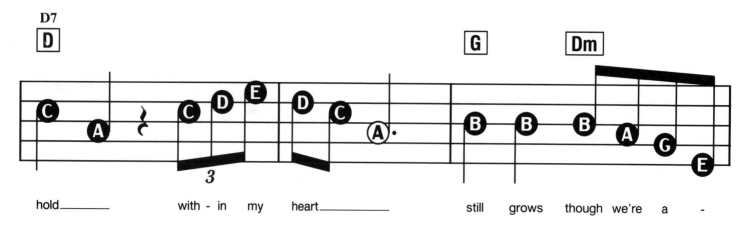
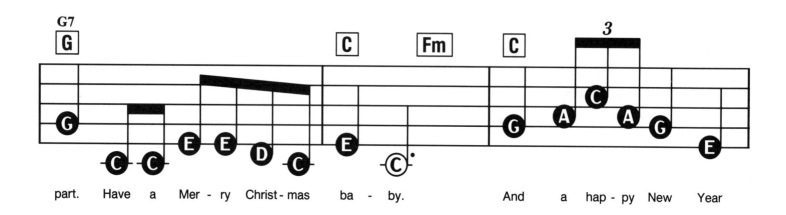
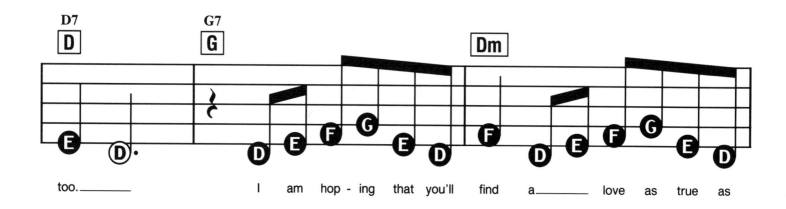
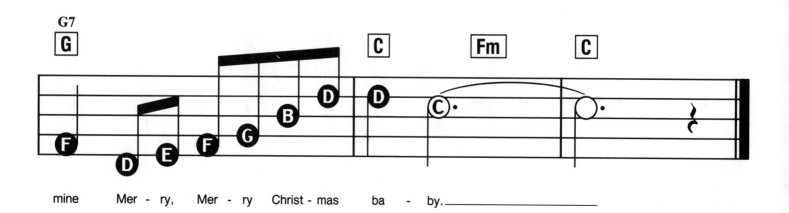

Shake Me I Rattle
(Squeeze Me I Cry)

Registration 3
Rhythm: Waltz

Words and Music by Hal Hackady
and Charles Naylor

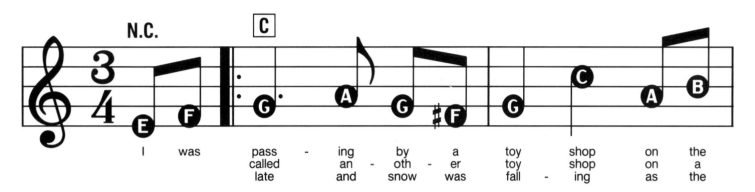

I was pass - ing by a toy shop on the
called an - oth - er toy shop on a
late and snow was fall - ing as the

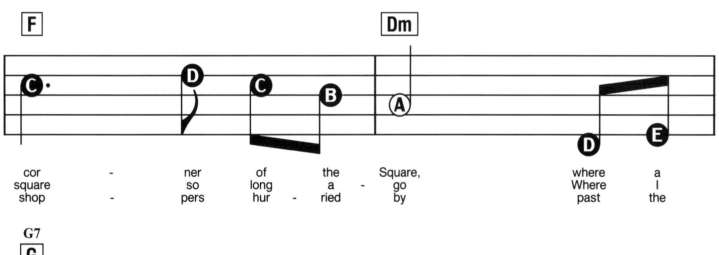

cor - ner of the Square, where a
square so long a - go Where I
shop - pers hur - ried by past the

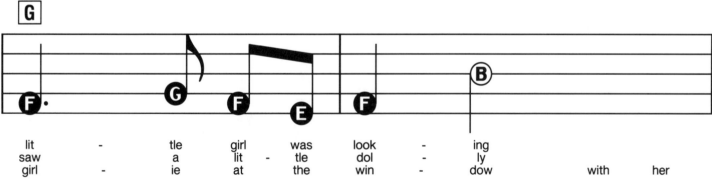

lit - tle girl was look - ing
saw a lit - tle dol - ly
girl - ie at the win - dow with her

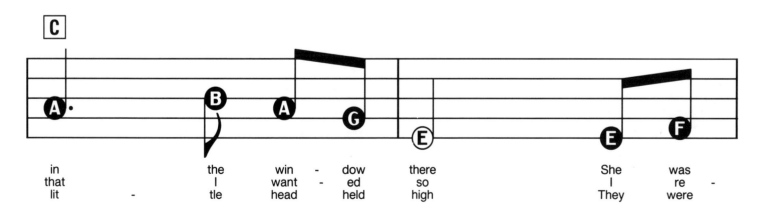

in the win - dow there She was
that I want - ed so I re -
lit - tle head held high They were

Copyright © 1957 (Renewed) by Regent Music Corporation
All Rights Reserved

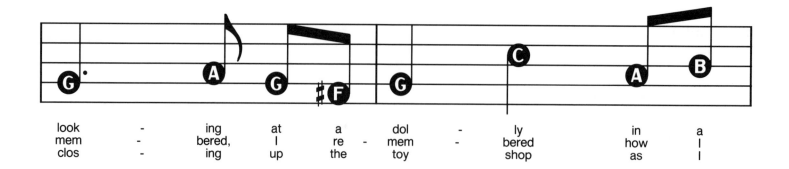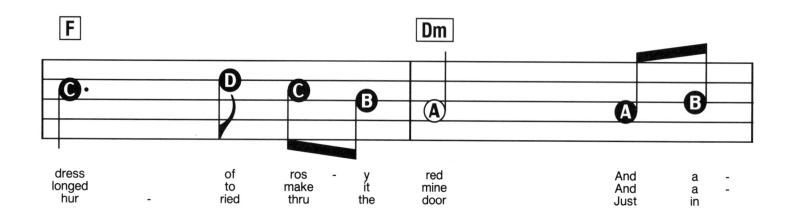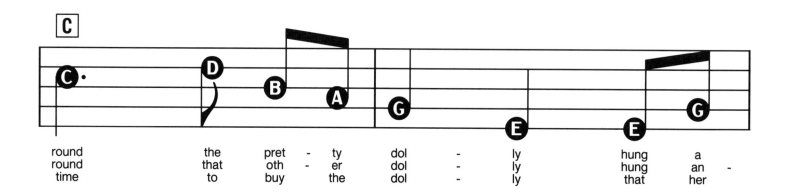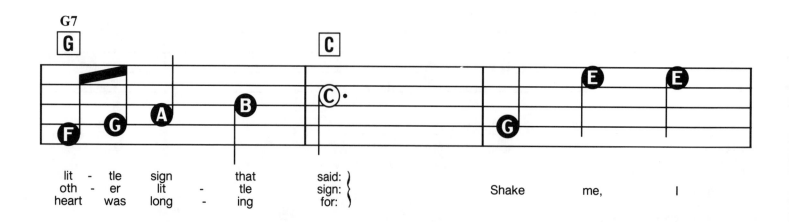

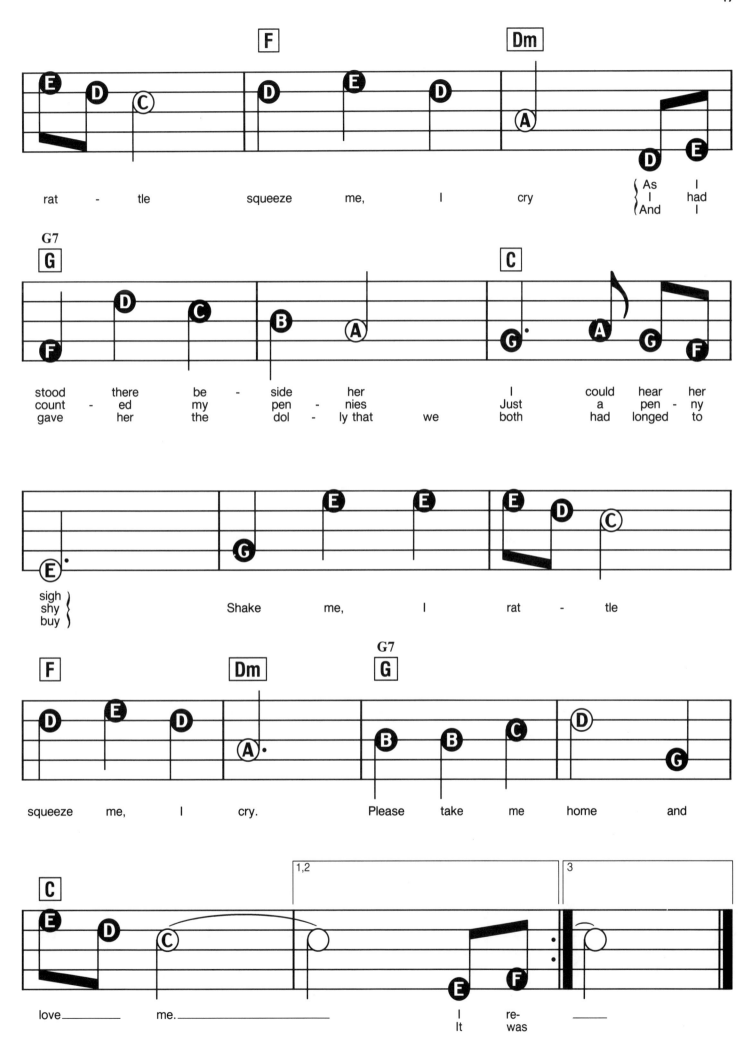

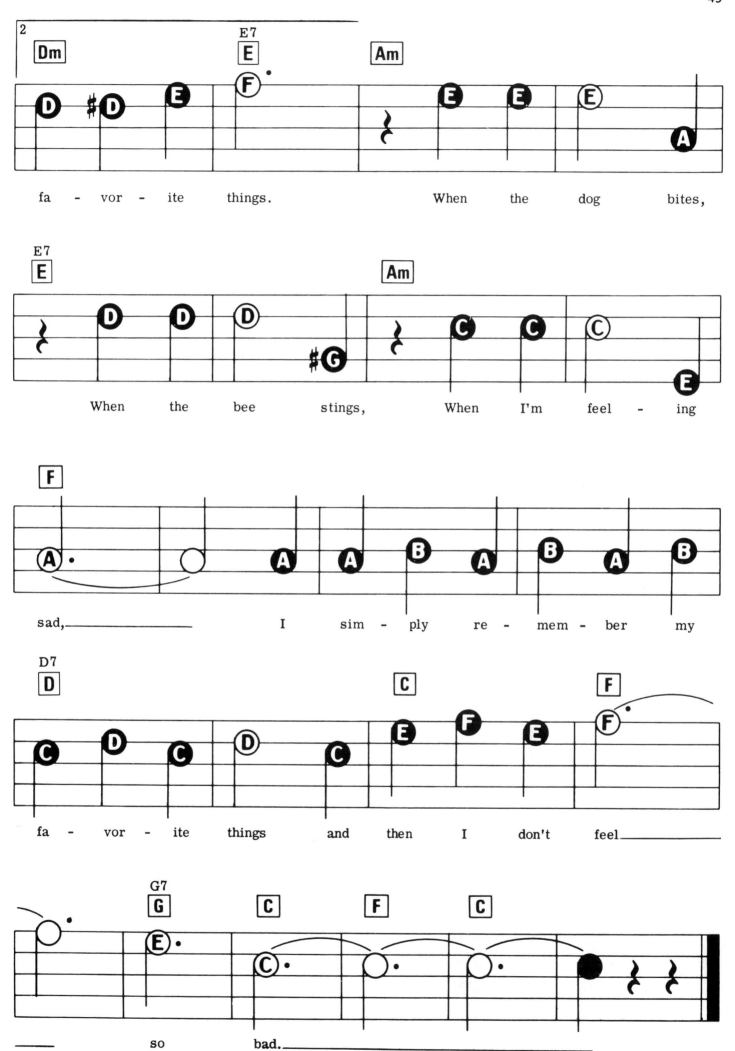

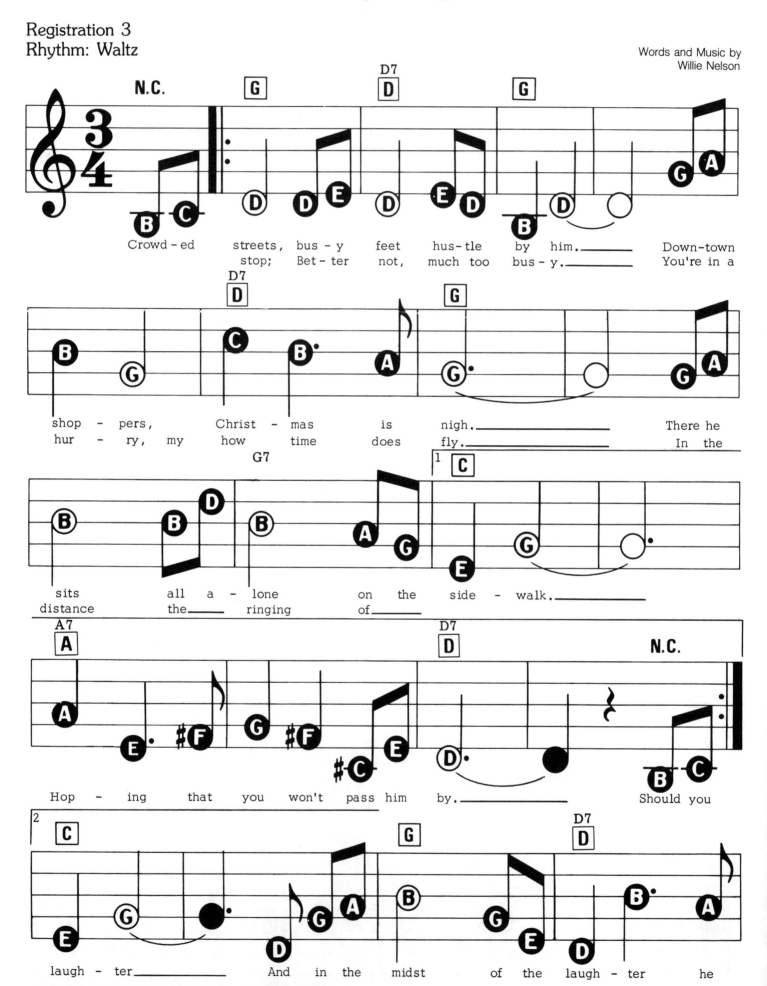

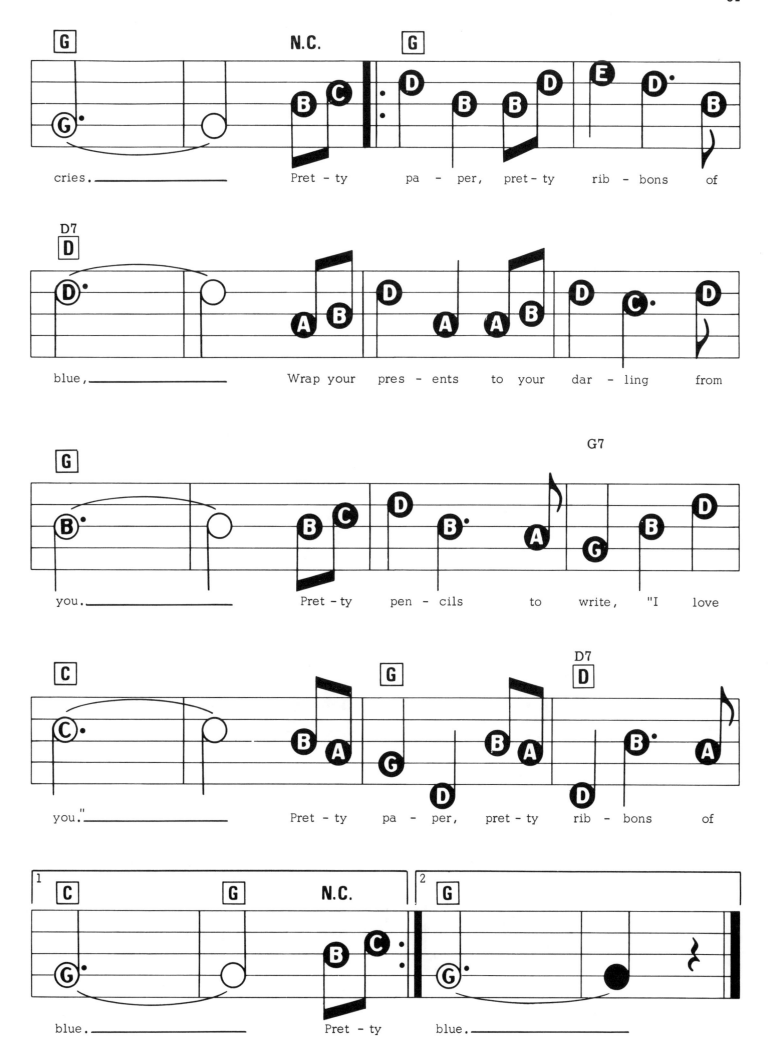

Rudolph The Red-Nosed Reindeer

Registration 4
Rhythm: Fox Trot or Swing

Music and Lyrics by
Johnny Marks

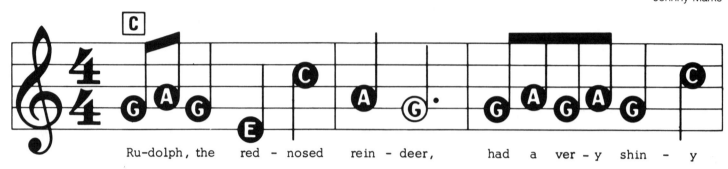
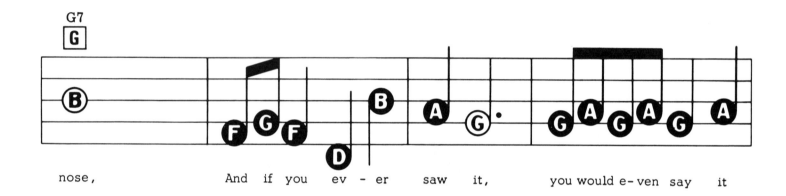
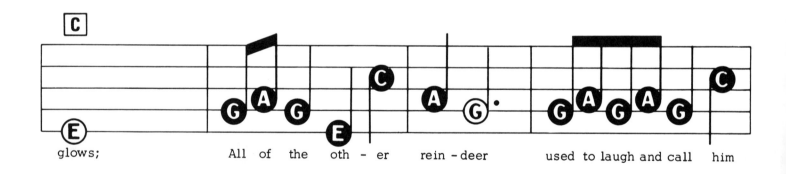
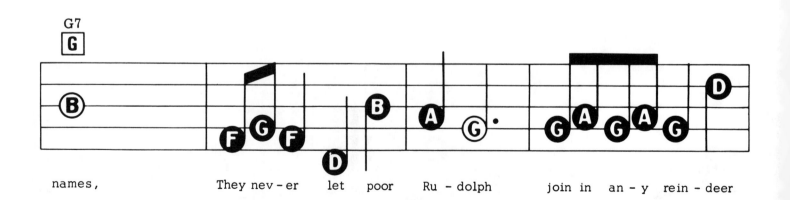

Copyright © 1949, Renewed 1977 St. Nicholas Music Inc., 1619 Broadway, New York, New York 10019
All Rights Reserved

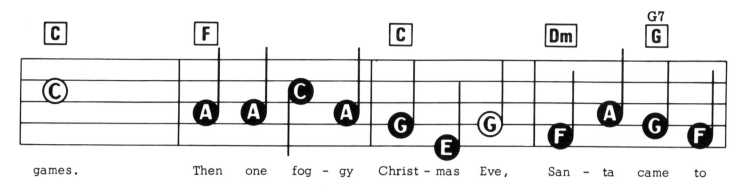
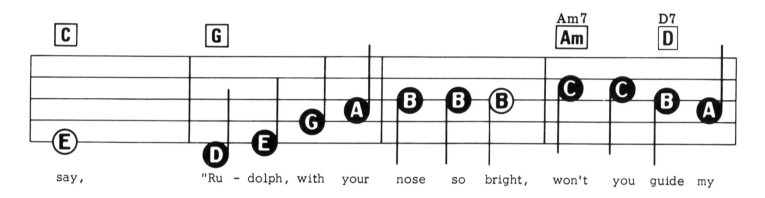
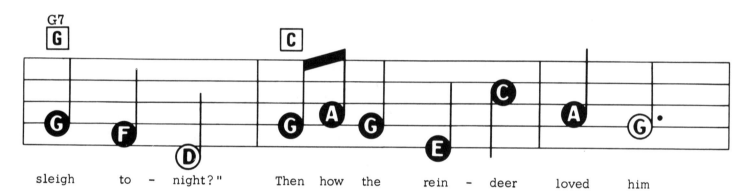
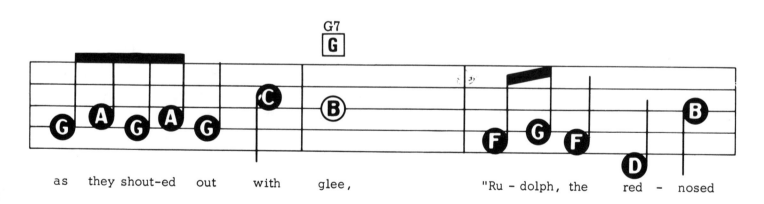
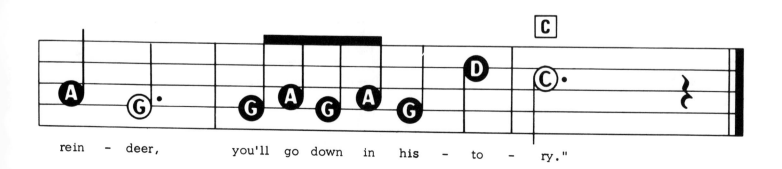

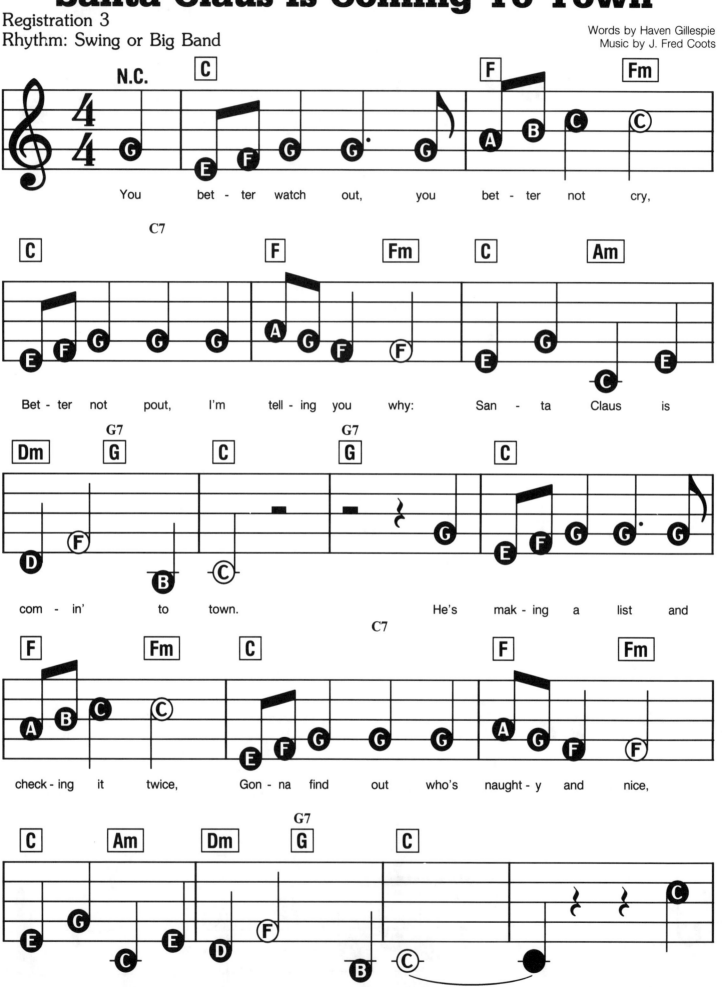

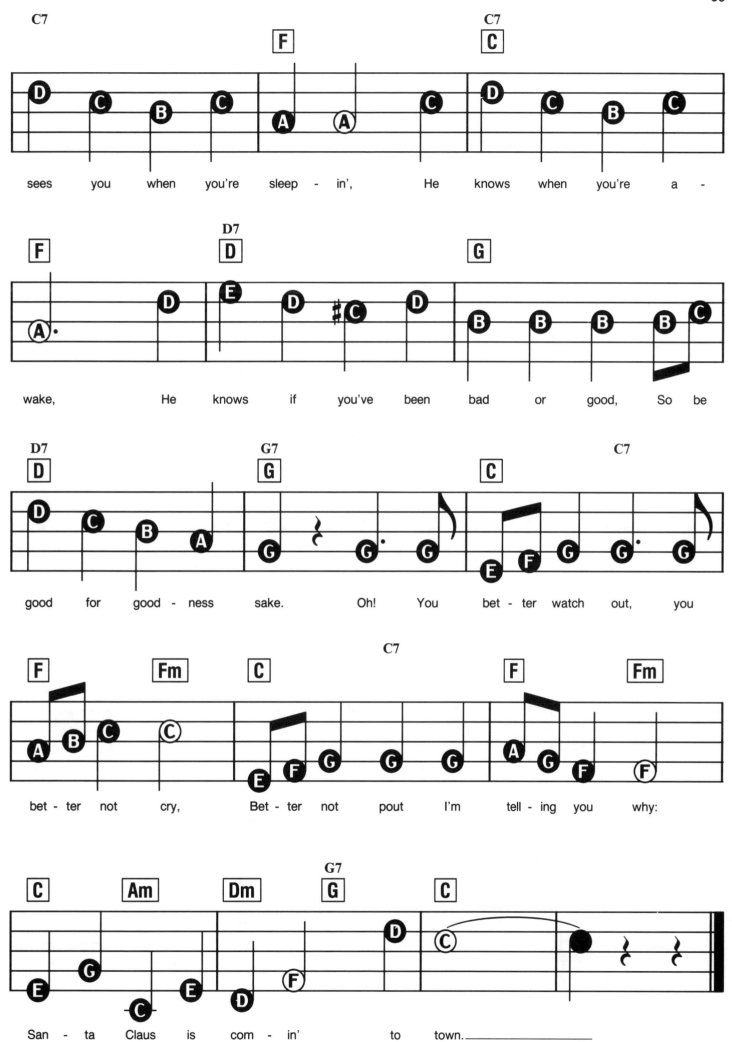

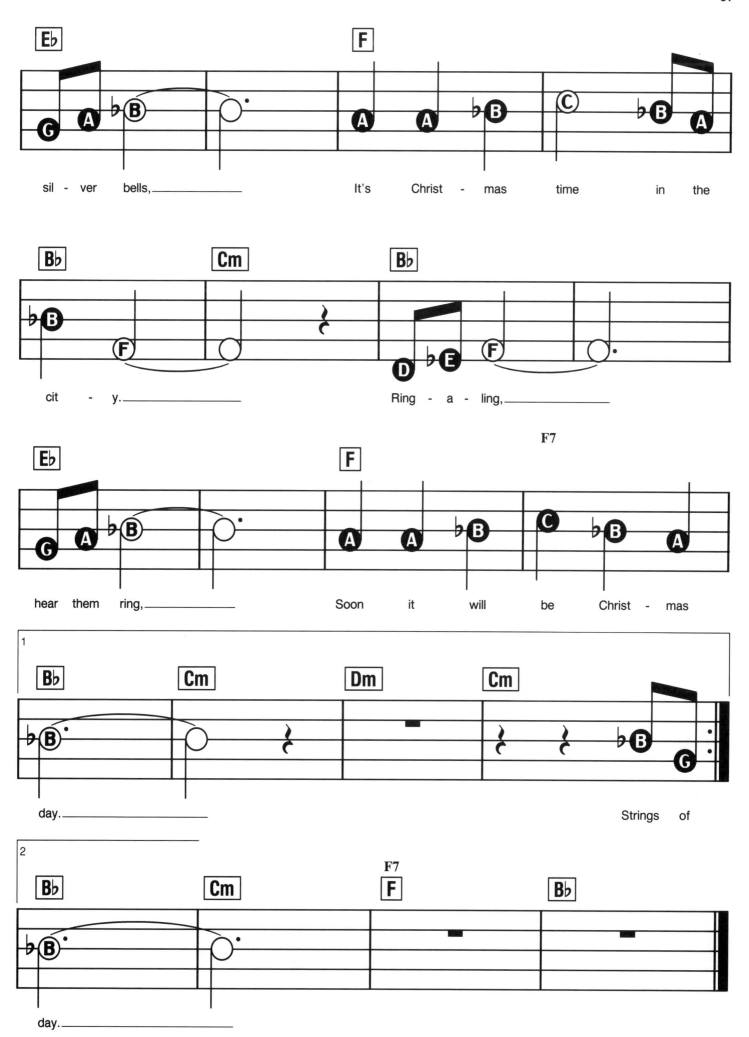

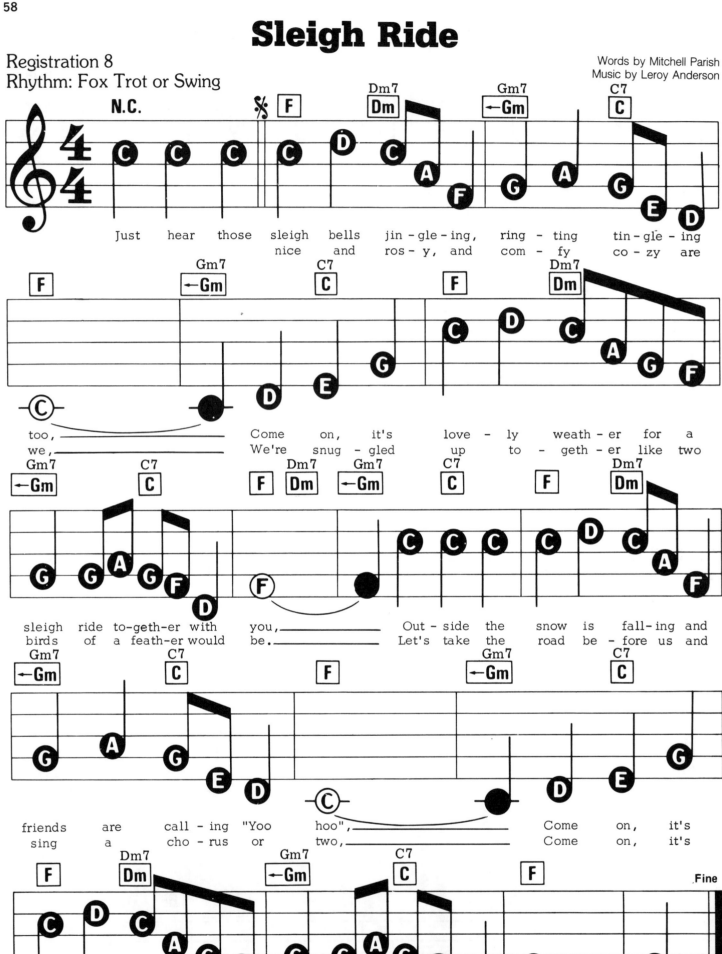

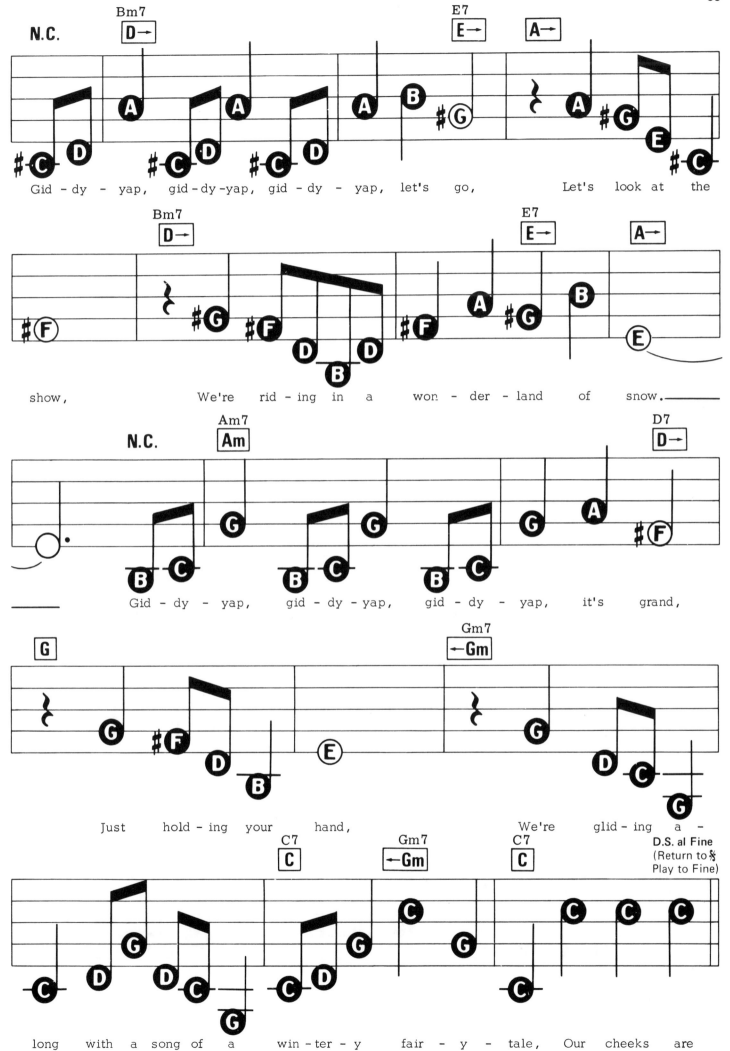

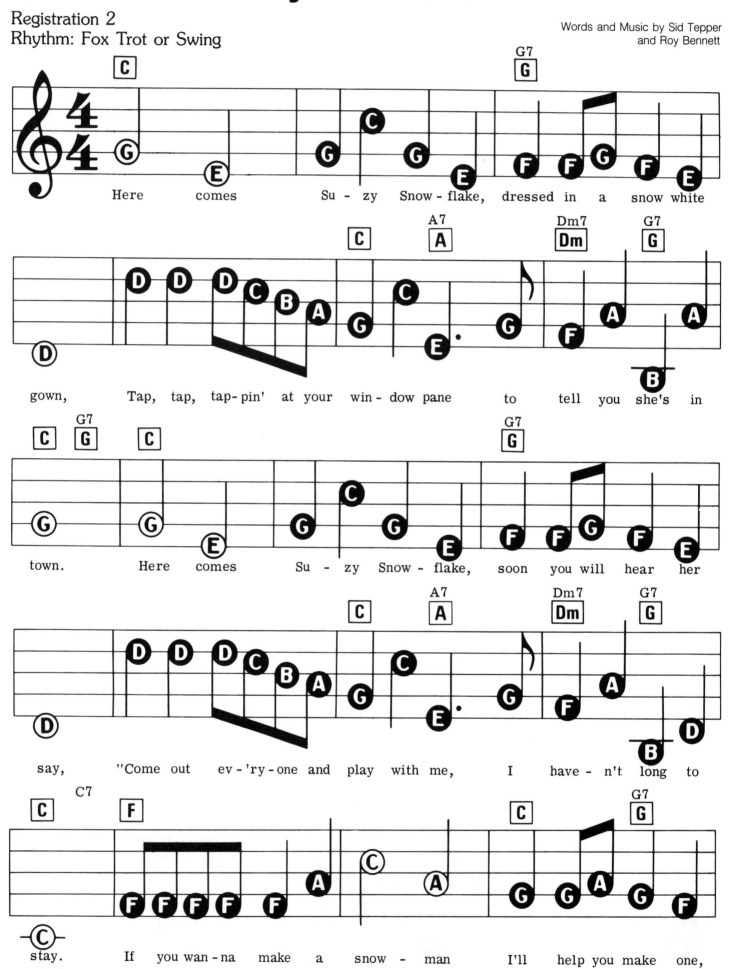

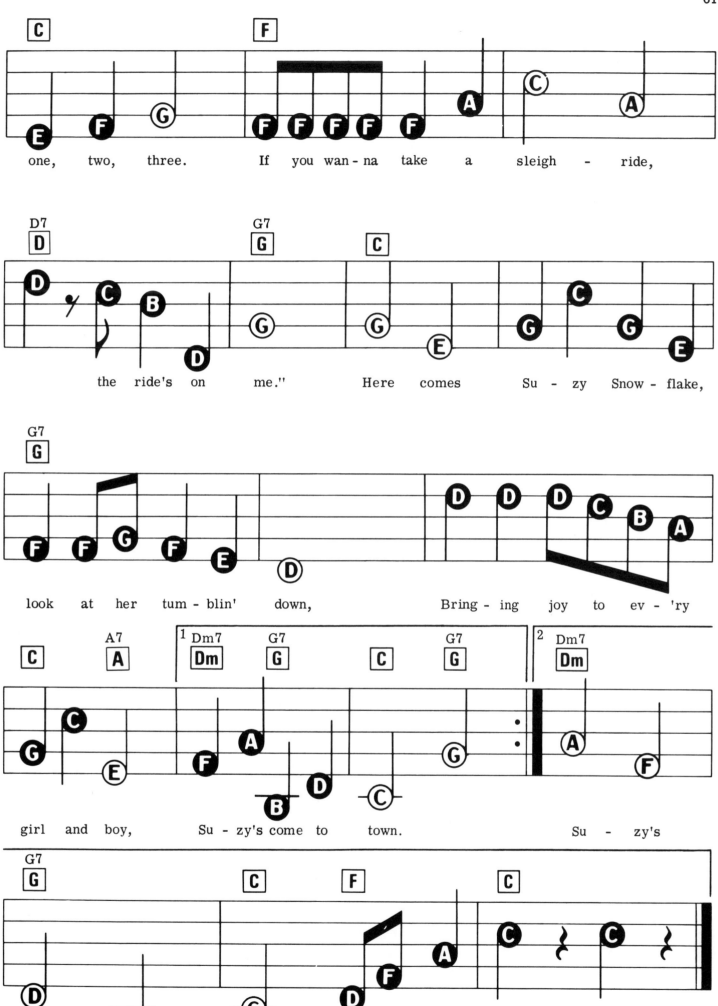

E-Z Play® TODAY Registration Guide For All Organs

On the following chart are 10 numbered registrations for both tonebar (TB) and electronic tab organs. The numbers correspond to the registration numbers on the E-Z Play TODAY songs. Set up as many voices and controls listed for each specific number as you have available on your instrument. For more detailed registrations, ask your dealer for the E-Z Play TODAY Registration Guide for your particular organ model.

REG. NO.		UPPER (SOLO)	LOWER (ACCOMPANIMENT)	PEDAL	GENERALS
1	Tab	Flute 16', 2'	Diapason 8' Flute 4'	Flute 16', 8'	Tremolo/Leslie – Fast
	TB	80 0808 000	(00) 7600 000	46, Sustain	Tremolo/Leslie – Fast (Upper/Lower)
2	Tab	Flute 16', 8', 4', 2', 1'	Diapason 8' Flute 8', 4'	Flute 16' String 8'	Tremolo/Leslie – Fast
	TB	80 7806 004	(00) 7503 000	46, Sustain	Tremolo/Leslie – Fast (Upper/Lower)
3	Tab	Flute 8', 4', 2⅔', 2' String 8', 4'	Diapason 8' Flute 4' String 8'	Flute 16', 8'	Tremolo/Leslie – Fast
	TB	40 4555 554	(00) 7503 333	46, Sustain	Tremolo/Leslie – Fast (Upper/Lower)
4	Tab	Flute 16', 8', 4' Reed 16', 8'	Flute 8', (4) Reed 8'	Flute 8' String 8'	Tremolo/Leslie – Fast
	TB	80 7766 008	(00) 7540 000	54, Sustain	Tremolo/Leslie – Fast (Upper/Lower)
5	Tab	Flute 16', 4', 2' Reed 16', 8' String 8', 4'	Diapason 8' Reed 8' String 4'	Flute 16', 8' String 8'	Tremolo/Leslie
	TB	40 4555 554 Add all 4', 2' voices	(00) 7503 333	57, Sustain	
6	Tab	Flute 16', 8', 4' Diapason 8' String 8'	Diapason 8' Flute 8' String 4'	Diapason 8' Flute 8'	Tremolo/Leslie – Slow (Chorale)
	TB	45 6777 643	(00) 6604 020	64, Sustain	Tremolo/Leslie – Slow (Chorale)
7	Tab	Flute 16', 8', 5⅓', 2⅔', 1'	Flute 8', 4' Reed 8'	Flute 8' String 8'	Chorus (optional) Perc Attack
	TB	88 0088 000	(00) 4333 000	45, Sustain	Tremolo/Leslie – Slow (Chorale)
8	Tab	Piano Preset or Flute 8' or Diapason 8'	Diapason 8'	Flute 8'	
	TB	00 8421 000	(00) 4302 010	43, Sustain	Perc Piano
9	Tab	Clarinet Preset or Flute 8' Reed 16', 8'	Flute 8' Reed 8'	Flute 16', 8'	Vibrato
	TB	00 8080 840	(00) 5442 000	43, Sustain	Vibrato
10	Tab	String (Violin) Preset or Flute 16' String 8', 4'	Flute 8' Reed 8'	Flute 16', 8'	Vibrato or Delayed Vibrato
	TB	00 7888 888	(00) 7765 443	57, Sustain	Vibrato or Delayed Vibrato

NOTE: TIBIAS may be used in place of FLUTES. VIBRATO may be used in place of LESLIE.

KEYBOARD ALPHABETICAL SONGFINDER

Complete listing of over 3000 songs included in the E-Z Play TODAY Songbook Series, SOLO TODAY, ORGAN ADVENTURE, EASY ELECTRONIC KEYBOARD MUSIC and PORTABLE KEYBOARD MUSIC Series. Song titles are cross-referenced to the books in which they can be found.

Available free of charge from your local music store. Or, write to:

HAL LEONARD PUBLISHING CORP.
P.O. Box 13819, Milwaukee, WI 53213

Ask for #90500057.